*Is Being*

    *A Wife*

        *A Part-Time Job?*

No way, says Oleda Baker—and she speaks from experience. Being both a top model *and* a good wife was never easy. Most of the time, the combination was simply impossible.

Eventually, Oleda realized that no professional success can provide a woman with the deep, abiding satisfaction of loving—and being loved.

BE A WOMAN! instructs you in the art of being a wife. It shows you how to find real fulfillment through another, caring person and deals frankly with the sacrifices you must often make for him.

A very special feature is the Complete Woman Analysis Chart, with which you can accurately evaluate your Feminine Growth Potential.

Now, in one invaluable book, learn what has taken many other women years to discover:

*Marriage Is The Ultimate Liberation*

# Be

# *A*

# *Woman!*

## Oleda Baker

BALLANTINE BOOKS • NEW YORK

SBN 345-24519-9-150

First Printing: June, 1975

Printed in the United States of America

BALLANTINE BOOKS
A Division of Random House, Inc.
201 East 50th Street, New York, N.Y. 10022
Simultaneously published by
Ballantine Books, Ltd., Toronto, Canada

This book is dedicated to all women who know the joy of being women. And especially dedicated to my dear friend Vernice Gabriel, whose advice and critical judgment were of enormous help to me during the writing of this book.

# Contents

# Introduction

FOR SEVERAL YEARS I was a successful New York model. My face was seen on national magazine covers and in TV commercials. I was taken to all the fashionable restuarants. I met and knew many celebrities.

But I wasn't a *complete* woman. It took me a long time to find out that being a wife and a mother was the most important element in my life.

Too many women are being misled today. Television, newspapers, books and magazines are delivering the message to us: the female revolution is here—we are to be liberated. But liberated from what? From our families? From our rightful roles as wives and mothers? From our husbands who complete us, as God meant them to?

Women's lives are meaningful when we fulfill our need to love—and to be loved. We are all free individuals, living in a free society. And we should be able to choose how we lead our lives. We should not be made to feel incomplete because we are not conforming to someone else's picture of what a woman should be.

I am writing this book for all the women who are being pressured into feeling inadequate, for all the women who are being made to feel ashamed and guilty because they truly *want* to be wives and mothers. This book is for those of you who want to fulfill yourselves within the home and not be competitive, unisex creatures in the outside world.

You, as a woman, do not have to have an affair,

or take a job, or burn your brassière. You can and should be proud of your purely female role.

Let your entire attitude, personality, and outlook spring from your feminine instincts. Feel comfortable needing and wanting a man.

By being born a woman you have an incredible advantage. You have a life that can provide you with the best of everything.

# 1

# How Lucky Can You Get?

As THE FEMALE half of a marriage, you are automatically endowed with an infinite variety of choices. Your life is far more flexible than that of your over-worked-nine-to-five-who-can-be-fired-at-any-time husband.

Men don't have the benefits of working at home. You can listen to the radio or stereo while working; watch TV whenever you wish; eat or munch at your leisure; take a nap "on company time"; call or visit your friends whenever you like; or take a day off once in a while. Did you ever stop to think that while he's there fighting for the money, you can spend the day at the beauty parlor or shopping for niceties?

You even have the time to take up a hobby, do volunteer work, join a dance class, or go swimming at the Y—in other words, do anything you choose, simply for the pleasure and satisfaction it gives you. And you don't *have* to deal with people you don't like. What man has this kind of freedom?

If a problem crops up that you can't handle, your husband is expected to take over. You, being a woman, are not expected to solve *every* problem. Your pride is not at stake. But to whom can he turn when confronted with a frustrating situation or a big decision that must be made? You can break down, cry, complain without being considered a weakling as a man would be. And all this without the pressures of earning a living!

All that is asked of you is that you keep yourself attractive to him, be a good sex partner, feed him when he's hungry, make sure the house is clean, see that the children are cared for, and give him the ego boost he needs by responding to him with respect and understanding.

Compare that list of responsibilities with your poor husband's. As the male of the species, he has been conditioned to the role of provider for his family. He has no pleasure options on company time. He has to compete every day, often doing work he doesn't enjoy. He must pay taxes and insurance premiums—his thinking ahead will provide for you even after his death. In addition, he must be ready to fight our wars and set a good example as a responsible citizen. No wonder a man has such a demanding ego.

Now, what woman would want to change places with a man? Not me!

How lucky can you get—to have someone whose instincts tell him to take care of you. That, in turn, should make you want to take care of him, but in your own feminine, womanly way. Your man needs you to fill his voids. His voids are where you shine most. That's the way God planned it. That's the way you should keep it.

## Estrogen versus Testosterone

Many people today are claiming that social conditioning has *taught* that the male and female roles are distinct from one another; that these roles are not predetermined; that society is supposedly responsible for creating artificial differences between men and women. If, so the argument goes, we weren't forced to believe from the cradle to the grave that women should stay at home and be wives and mothers while men should go out into the world, there would be no difference between the sexes. I don't accept this argument.

There are definite biological differences between the male and the female. Testosterone, the male hormone, is responsible for masculine characteristics. Estrogen, the female hormone, gives a woman her feminine distinctions.

There are also emotional and intellectual differences. And it is the differences that make life so beautiful and fascinating. How dull it would be if we were all the same!

From a therapeutic point of view, both men and women should accept the behavioral patterns that society has created and accepted for thousands of years. It seems that too many people today want to tear down the system that God arranged from the beginning of time, instead of working positively within it.

No complete woman wants to fight with her complete man for equal time at the make-up mirror, or over who should change the oil in the car, or who's going to give the baby his bottle. Nature is arbitrary; it doesn't intend for us to split our personalities or our responsibilities. Just as man and woman fit together physically to create a unity, so they should fit together to fulfill each other's needs. That's being practical as well as natural—and anyway it's more fun.

3

## *My Life Wouldn't Be Complete Without Him*

The most beautiful experience in life is knowing and feeling the joy of being a woman.

What *is* the joy of being a woman? For me the joy starts when I get up in the morning—and it goes on into my dreams at night. The first joy is seeing my husband still asleep in the morning, to know he was beside me all night. To see his sleepy smile as he wakes, and to know that I have contributed to that smile. When I see him in the shower, his body so different from mine, I exult in his masculinity.

The joy is making our bed in the morning, thinking of the day ahead as his wife, and looking forward to the night with him. When he goes off to the office, I am secure, warm with knowing that he is both protector and provider.

The joy is taking care of the daily routine at home, creating a relaxing atmosphere for us to enjoy together. My joy is seeing his eyes light up with that special message when he returns from his day in the jungle: "It's good to be home and I'm happy you're here."

My joy is privacy with him, to know that he needs me, too. When he takes me in his arms and says "I couldn't do it without you," that's my reward—my joy. My life wouldn't be complete without him!

I'm not unique in this respect; for women who are adjusted and happy with themselves, the most rewarding experience is sharing life with another. And it is natural that she should want to share her experiences with a man. We learn from the Bible that the first woman was created from a rib of the first man. From

4

that moment, woman has thus been an extension of man.

One of the signs of advanced civilization is the institution of marriage. It has had its ups and downs through the years—it's certainly being attacked today. But somehow, it always seems to emerge intact. It's no doubt one of the strongest bonds that has existed, exists, and will exist between two people. Maybe that's nature's way of propagating the species, or maybe it's God's expression of the highest form of love. Be that as it may—it works.

I believe I speak not only for myself but for every woman blessed with the basic drives of her sex when I say that being part of a man is being wholly a woman. This is an emotional fact that has God's blessing. "Woman cannot do without a man," says the Bible; "neither can man do without woman, in the Lord." A woman's love for a man is as much of her being as her entire anatomy.

I have also found that a woman who shares her life with a man is so much happier. She feels complete and acts the part. An inner joy, a sense of fulfillment, shows in her face, her smile, her way of talking, and in her marvelous capacity for enjoyment of life. More often than not, the best wife makes the best mother, relative, and friend. She relates to people better and is better able to withstand the pressures and tensions of everyday living. The reason is simple enough: she always has someone to fall back on, talk to, love, and be loved by.

And don't ever minimize the importance of love. It is a two-way street and *both* directions are important! At the expense of sounding obvious, I would like to remind you that giving love can be just as fulfilling as receiving love. It is one of the richest experiences a woman can have—loving her husband.

5

A giving woman seems more complete to the outside world—she functions better, looks better, acts more wisely. But more important, she has a profound feeling of peace that stems from knowing that she is complete. Her good feelings will be returned from her husband, just as a joyful shout will bounce back from the walls of a mountainside.

Remember that Christ said, "Give and ye shall receive." If a woman gives herself to her husband, supports him totally, she has been promised a gift from God, a gift that will make for a most tranquil and tender relationship.

## The Long-Range Female Perspective

There are times in life when you feel frustrated and trapped—when the children are in their early years, for example. Your time is filled with their demands, in addition to your household chores and caring for your husband. The female role seems suddenly overwhelming. But learning to consider these problem periods from a long-range point of view—as only *part* of an eighty-year life span—will help you get through them. You will see that they are really only a fraction of your entire life.

Your life is divided into three parts:

*The first twenty years (birth to marriage).* You are free of any responsibilities of providing for others. *You* are the one provided for.

*The next twenty years (marriage to weaning of children).* You are asked to contribute to others (your husband and children) while still taking care of your own needs. Remember, this relatively short span in your life should be enjoyed, problems and all. It will form a rich part of your fondest memories one day.

*The next forty years* (golden years—"Life begins

at forty"). The "hard" years are behind you. Experience has enriched you, and it is your turn once again to indulge in your pleasures. You have only your husband and yourself to care for. He will still pamper, protect, and provide for you, and ask only that his needs be fulfilled in return.

Thus there are only twenty years (one-quarter of your life) when you are expected to extend yourself for the concentrated care of others, and sixty years (three-quarters of your life) when you can be self-indulgent.

Compared with the male, who has to work from the end of schooling to retirement (approximately sixty years) in order to support himself and his family, I think the female, *you,* is by far the luckier.

# 2

# *Your Marvelous Man*

## *Man—The Endangered Species*

WELL, WE'VE been blasé about some of the world's animals and plants, taking them for granted, feeling they will always be there—and they have become extinct, never to be duplicated again. Are we going to just stand by and let the human male become extinct, too? If we don't stand up for him—allow him to keep his masculinity and love him the way he is—he may very well become extinct. Okay, so his body will still be around, but *he* will not be the species we know today. He'll have different instincts, different feelings, different goals—and his view of women will be different.

When you try to change your man's habits or character, you are doing nothing more than selfishly trying to have your own way. Your endangered species is not expected to look at the world through your eyes, have your reactions and standards. The more he is expected to, the more endangered he'll become.

A woman is happy and feels confident when she is performing her role as she *knows* it to be. All cultures have traditionally accepted and enjoyed the male as the dominant, aggressive, stronger counterpart for many ages. The male is comfortable with his role, which gives him the security to handle major, over-all responsibilities. I want my man to keep those responsibilities. God gave them to him but, at the same time, made it easy for him by giving him the instincts and abilities necessary to fulfill those responsibilities. I was attracted to my husband in the first place because I enjoyed his masculinity. I like his identity and I am tolerant of his idiosyncrasies. But if I were to try to establish my independence by competing on his level, I would threaten his security as a male. So I let him feel secure in his masculinity (and I remind him of it daily), and he, in turn, sees me as very feminine and keeps me on a pedestal. And you know what? I like it there.

Children learn their male/female roles by emulating their parents. If they grow up in a family where the mother and father are competing with each other, how will they know what is feminine or masculine? In time, the male/female roles might be *reversed*. Do we really want that? I certainly don't! But the problem isn't created by the women who enjoy their female role; it's created by women who are confused. If a few women want to assert themselves, it's all right with me, but I don't agree with either their approach or their ultimate goal, which seems to be to make *all* women feel the pressure to change, to perform.

Women's liberation is getting so much publicity in the U.S. that both men and women are confused now. In other countries, where the movement has not yet taken hold there are fewer divorces because those women accept their roles and allow the men to remain secure in their masculinity. There must be areas of awe and mystery on both sides or else the fascination each sex has for the other dissipates. So understand your man and respect him for his role in life.

I would like to answer women's lib by organizing the women who feel as I do and march us up every main street in the country with our message: "We Like Our Men the Way They Are!" In the meantime, we can use that slogan in our daily contacts. If you find it hard to say, write it and then tape it to his bathroom mirror or his dresser. He'll go out into the world that day with his chin, even his nose, up in the air. If each one of you would tell your man, we could cover most of the males around. *Start today!* Put your man back in the driver's seat and insure his existence as the adoring, strong protector.

## Understanding Him

Men didn't get the way they are overnight. They've had thousands of years of conditioning, learning to be men.

It all started in the Garden with Eve. Adam took a bite of the apple and man has had problems ever since. What did he know? It was a brand-new experience for him and there was no one to advise him otherwise.

Then there was Salomé, who used her feminine arts to get the head of John the Baptist.

Cleopatra went a step further. With her feminine trickery, she beguiled and then destroyed the most powerful men of her era, precipitating the downfall of empires.

And when settlers first came to this country, the female/male ratio was 1 to 10. The female had to be protected; she was in *over*-demand.

Today, men are dumfounded by the brash outspokenness of some women in the public eye. Because of their conditioned respect for womanhood, they don't even fight back. The women take advantage of this respect inherent in men to get what they want. Our poor men don't have a chance.

This female instinct to dominate has parallels in the world of insects—the queen bee, for instance, uses her male lover once and he's dead; the female spider traps her lover, uses him, then eats him.

It's time *now* to give men a chance. From the very first moment a man is born, he has women telling him what to do. Naturally, he needs his mother in infancy and early childhood. Then, when he starts school, he, more than likely, has a female teacher instructing him. Yet, in this world of female domination, he is expected to be masculine in every way; if he is not, he is kidded by his peers or, worse, not accepted. If he makes top grades in school, he is suspect. If he loves classical music, he is suspect. His masculinity is measured by his peers by the size of his penis; he worries about his ability to perform sexually—not just *will* he be able to, but *how* well he'll be able to.

How, then, do men turn out to be mature, responsible, and rational adults? Answer: by a good relationship with an understanding woman, by her faith in him and his masculinity. Before he met you, your man probably suffered the ego bruises of domination or rejection from other women. He needs you to cure his self-doubts—to help prove his manhood. That's probably what made him fall in love with you in the first place. Now, if you want to keep him for life, then it's a lifetime job. Don't slack off after ten years and wonder why he is looking at, or for, other women. It's natural for a man to need reassurance; he must keep his self-confidence up. If you don't help, another woman will—believe it!

If you understand your man to the fullest degree, the rewards are tremendous. He will believe in himself, and that will turn him on to you. He will talk *with* you, not at you. If you give him confidence and attention, he will be able to meet the world halfway. While he's out struggling with his job during the day, he will think of his woman back home, waiting for him, believing in him. That's a lot to come home to.

Your man has his head full of demands he must meet if he is to retain his virility. No wonder he acts strangely sometimes! It's an effort to keep it all together at *all* times—and that's where you come in. You can help him keep it together by understanding him. Sounds simple? Well, it's not!

A man has a deep emotional need to be known and understood by a woman. He has to feel you understand him totally. Along with understanding goes acceptance and need. He needs you, *and he needs you to need him*—that's how he bolsters his self-image. He needs to feel that he is a responsible mate, fulfilling the needs of his woman. This is basic to understanding the male psyche. Your man doesn't like to feel that you can get along without him. Needing him sexually is the department of most concern to him, and it infiltrates all the rest of his thinking. A man wants his woman to *need* him—not just tolerate him —in every area—sexual satisfaction, protection, and financial support. If you *need* your man enough, he will be everything manly you could desire.

## Support Your Local Man

How many times have you gone out to support a local friend or politician? Remember how grateful he was for your help? You did whatever was asked of you with eagerness, and you believed in what he said and did.

Think what would happen if you supported *your*

"local man" with the same enthusiasm. He would be ardently grateful. He would develop into the best friend you ever had, as well as being president of your heart and home.

Your man needs to be supported just the way he is. He likes what he is and nothing you say or do will change him; trying to change him may bring out the worst in him, and you might lose him. Steve, for example, is a very private person, even somewhat of an introvert. No amount of trying to change him into a party type will make him so. Instead, I look at the positive side. The fact that he is a private person makes him more of a homebody and partner to me. Which means I see more of him.

Even if the worst doesn't happen, trying to change your man will make him resent and even rebel against you. And why shouldn't he? Would you like to have someone constantly finding fault with you and trying to change your ways? You naturally want people to like you as you are. So, the first step is to support your husband *unconditionally*. No games—no deals. Your rewards will follow naturally. He will respond by trying to please you, to show you his appreciation.

If he knows you support him, he will feel free to confide in you, to pour his heart out to you, to be himself. He can't really be himself outside your home, so if you want to see him rush home to you in the evening, give him the pleasure of accepting him as he is. Listen to him—from the heart.

If you truly want to support your man, here's where to start:

*No Nagging*. Nagging is the opposite of accepting. If you nag your man, you are not accepting him. For instance, if he leaves the cap off the toothpaste, so what? It's his toothpaste, too. It's not going to turn green overnight. Are you going to let a toothpaste

13

cap come between you? It's his home, and he should
feel free to live as he wants. If he drinks, smokes,
works too hard, no amount of nagging will help him.
In fact, all that plus nagging will send him to the
grave earlier. If you want a warm and happy relationship, concentrate on all his good qualities—he
may even stop nagging you about the amount of
money you spend!

*Accept Him.* Don't try to change him. Look back
to the time before you married him—he was basically
the same then as now. You saw his idiosyncracies
and you overlooked them; sometimes you probably
thought of them as cute or part of his charm. Why
should you see him differently now? You married
him, but that does not give you the right to change
him. If you wanted something different, you should
have married someone else.

Years ago, a friend of mine married a shy, rather
quiet young man, a lawyer. Les wasn't pushy or loud;
he was the kind of man who just goes ahead and gets
a job done. He felt most comfortable behind the
scenes instead of hogging the courtroom spotlight. It
wasn't as though he didn't make a nice income, or that
he wasn't a loving husband, but my friend felt that
he was hiding his light. He tried to explain to her that
he *wanted* to hide his light . . . that he'd rather do
the backroom work and let the others take the bows.
But my friend wouldn't have it. She prodded and
nagged him, ridiculed and belittled him. Well, he
didn't turn out to be a Perry Mason, but he did become an ex-husband.

How foolish my friend was. She took stock of the
man she had married and came to a dangerous con-
clusion: he was okay to marry and, fine, I do love
him . . . but I need him to be a bigshot in the world's
eyes.

You can't do this. If you want your relationship with your husband to succeed, you *must* accept him. It's as simple as that. You will be a happier and better person for it. Living with resentment within yourself day after day will give a negative quality to your personality. It will begin to show on your face; every time he looks at you, he'll be reminded of your resentment.

*The Children Must Support Him, Too.* If your support is obvious, as it should be, your children will automatically pick it up. You can even suggest things they should do for their father. Like acknowledging him with a kiss or just a "Hi, Dad" when he comes home. And they could make sure the newspaper is in order—just as it was delivered—so he can get the most pleasure from reading it. If you serve him first at table, they see the respect you have for him. They should be taught that their father is the head of the family and deserves their respect. This is an excellent way for children to learn respect for others, which is part of what's missing in today's society.

How often I've seen children put ahead of the husband. That is really short-term thinking, and it affects everyone involved: the children get the impression they are more important than anyone else and therefore respect no one; your man will feel second-rate; you will lose the respect of both. Your man is a lifetime partner, and how you treat him in the family circle will affect your relationship with him later on, after the children are on their own.

Your children are not being neglected if they are taught that father comes first. It's the beginning of an important lesson in life.

*Don't Compare Him.* I'm sure you've heard many conversations between women comparing their men. I have a friend who is constantly raving about her girl friend's husband, who has a knack for making people feel at ease, and she wishes her husband could be the same way. I have reminded her that her own husband has a quality that many other wives would love their husbands to have—that of wanting to spend as much time with their children as possible. Another woman I know admires a neighbor who is handy around the house; she overlooks the social adeptness of her own man, who brings excitement to her life.

People are like snowflakes: no two are alike. Each individual is a separate, complex entity. No one is capable of excelling at *everything*—no one is complete perfection. That's what makes us mutually attractive, what binds our relationships. We are partially drawn to people who have the qualities or abilities we lack.

Take another look at your man. Remember what made you love him in the beginning. He fulfilled your needs, emotionally and physically. If you lost him, those needs would be exposed again. Take inventory of your wonderful man and appreciate his qualities; count your blessings. He shines where others don't and if you let him know you are aware of this, he will try even harder to make you happy.

*Admire Him.* A woman needs to be loved. A man needs to be admired. If you say to him "I love you," his answer will be short and simple—"I love you, too." Next time you plan a dinner for just the two of you, tell him how much you *admire* him—and be ready for a long conversation!

Admiring anything about him makes him happy—think of the qualities you admired in him many years ago, or maybe some new ones have developed. You may not believe this but men *still* want their physical strength to be admired by women. Now I know you are going to say you don't really care if your man has muscles. It's true that most women don't care. But it's not what *you* care about, it's what *he* cares about.

If you admire your man, do not interrupt his conversation. Give him your full attention. And *never* contradict what he is saying to someone else. He may have a reason for slanting a fact.

I remember a very unpleasant situation at a party. The guests were happily getting to know each other, and, as usual, the men were outdoing each other in the boasting game. Suddenly, one of the wives started contradicting what her husband was saying. She took the wind out of his sails, making him look like a liar. Needless to say, it put a damper on everyone's evening.

Another couple I know are a joy to be around. There is an aura about them of being in love. When they look at each other, their faces show their mutual respect and admiration. And when they speak of each other, it is always with an appreciation of the other's qualities and abilities. They've been married for fifteen years and I'm sure there must be disagreements between them, but they work them out *privately.*

Your husband is the most important person in your life and should be treated with respect and admiration above all others, in private and in public. Love and happiness are strengthened by a mutual respect and admiration. Support your man emotionally and he will love you more. He might even grow in areas you feel are important. In your appreciation of what he *is,* he will find the courage and inspiration to try to please you in every way.

## Should Your Husband Be Your Best Friend?

It seems to me that almost since the day I was born, I was raised to love my future husband—to be loyal and to generally care *for* him as well as *about* him.

As I grew into womanhood those values stayed with me. Even when I was modeling and living what many people regard as a glamorous, fulfilling life (it's really just hard work and very dull), I held on to those values. I saw many people ignoring what I had learned as a child—and what I knew to be right —and they were terribly unhappy. Happiness, it always seemed to me, was living under God's light and by the principles He set up, and, as a woman, being an understanding, loving wife and mother. I held on to my values and I'm not sorry.

A woman marries and plans to love her husband, to be a good sex partner, to be loyal, and to care for him in general. There is nothing wrong with that. But something is missing. *FRIENDSHIP!* I believe it is one of the most important elements in a relationship.

Your husband should be your best friend; you, in turn, will be his. But many people seem to overlook this. How often have you heard anyone refer to their wife or husband as their best friend? We just haven't been trained to think of a mate as a best friend. I certainly don't think it's a result of negative thinking on a woman's part. Rather, it is simply that few women have thought through the idea. Even at one of your happiest moments—when you were getting married—didn't you introduce as your best friend the maid of honor or one of the bridesmaids? You didn't mean it to be a put-down of your husband; but just think how proud he would have been if you had introduced him as your best friend.

Once in a while, you seen a married couple who, after twenty or thirty years, are still admiring each other. Well, the chances are that they are the best of friends, too. No marriage lasts if the wife doesn't treat her husband with the same respect and courtesy as she treats her best friend.

18

What exactly *is* a friend? To me it's someone I can go to for support or advice, that I have strong affection and high regard for. It's someone I can depend on and who, in turn, can depend on me. In *Webster's* a friend is defined as "one attached to another by respect and affection."

It *is* very possible to turn your husband into your best friend. But to keep him as such, you must learn how to constructively disagree with him. My own rule is to get it off my chest while the issue is small. Waiting only builds up resentment, and it can bring on either the silent treatment or an explosion. Your relationship should be open to frank but *friendly* conflicts.

I'm proud to say that my husband is my best friend and I am his. But this did not happen automatically. I worked at being his best friend by being there when he needed me and by taking an active interest in his world. He then found it natural to do the same. Our best-friendship is to our marriage like fertilizer is to a plant: it feeds the marriage, makes it grow and blossom, and keeps it strong and healthy. (I just checked with my husband to see if he objected to our friendship's being compared to fertilizer. He said, "From you, it's okay. From anyone else—I'd object." Now that's what I call a real friend!)

It's not too late to begin sharing experiences *as friends*. And, little by little, it will become an integral part of your marriage.

## Ways to Stay His Best Friend

No friendship will live forever unless it is rewarding to *both* parties. There has to be a mutual satisfaction of needs and a balance of give and take.

If you can:

1. put yourself in the other person's shoes and feel what he feels;

2. express your positive feelings about the other person;

3. be yourself—shed your masks and build a non-superficial honest relationship;

4. make the other person feel at ease;

you are well on your way to being a good friend to anyone—most of all to your husband.

A really good friendship is not easy to come by. One must work for it, and work to maintain it. Guard against indulging in suspicion or hostility; don't be calculating or devious. Instead, express affection and trust to your friend. Talk to him—show him that you care. Be the one to whom he can unburden his most secret thoughts. Be the one it's fun to be with, a pleasure to be around. No matter what you are talking about, strive to maintain an atmosphere of warmth and well-being.

A friend should be able to induce a feeling of satisfaction, of being wanted and needed. Give this to your husband and you'll have a friend for life.

If you are quarrelsome, nagging, irritable, overly demanding of attention, you are not best-friend material.

Here are some ways that will help you *stay* your husband's best friend for life:

1. *Know His Likes and Dislikes.* This applies to every department. If your likes are his dislikes, talk it over, bring all conflicts out into the open. Don't hide anything. But make sure it is an intelligent conversation, not an argument. Talk to him in the evening when he's relaxed and after the children are in bed. Keep your voice soft and be feminine. If you are shrill or demanding, you will turn him off.

2. *Learn More About His Occupation.* No matter

what it is. Find out about the history of his company, about his day-to-day activity, what the future possibilities are. Read books about it.

3. *Be Interested and, If Possible, Take Part in His Hobbies.* Help him whenever you can. Maybe offer to pick up an item he needs for his hobby. Whatever his hobby is, getting involved in it can teach you a lot, besides being fun. Get him interested in your hobby, even if it's only on a superficial basis. But don't bore him. Hobbies should be relaxing and fun. And remember, his hobby is *his*. Don't take it over. Your husband has enough competition on his job; he doesn't need more at home.

4. *Keep Up With or in Some Way Be Involved in, His Interests.* They can become yours, too. If they do, you will be the one he thinks of when he's involved with them. Maybe he talks a lot about history, music, cars, stocks, politics, philosophy. Whatever they are, know something about them. He will love being able to talk to you about his favorite subjects. My husband is in advertising, and he is always having to learn more about different types of products. So, as I read, I collect articles for him relating to whatever product he is working on. I also collect information on any other products I think he might want to know more about.

5. *Know His Friends.* At his job and otherwise. Tell him you would like to have a party for his friends. Get to know them. Make them *your* friends, too—but don't take them over. He would resent monopoly, just as you would.

6. *Chip in and Help When He Needs You.* Just as you would for your best girl friend. If he's doing a repair job in the house, for instance, help him. Not only will he appreciate your help and interest, but you will have more time with him. If you are there

when he needs you (even if it's only to hand him a wrench), you'll find he will be around when you need him. That's one thing friends are for.

7. *If He's an Outdoorsman, Learn to Enjoy Them With Him.* You, too, can love gardening, sports, flying, horses, et cetera. If you don't, somebody else will.

The whole idea is to be interested in his interests so you can share the fun together. You will find communication comes much easier when you are both on the same wave length. By your willingness to learn about *his* world, you will find that *your* world is expanded; *best of all,* you will have your husband to share it with.

Be his helpmate, for as God says in Genesis, "It is not good that man should be alone. I will make a help meet for him." And so Eve came into being.

## *Do You Take Your Husband for Granted?*

I know, I can hear it now—"But my husband takes me for granted, too!" That's exactly how I felt. But I have learned the hard way that if I don't take him for granted he, in turn, can't take me for granted. I mean, if I tell him for months how much I appreciate his ability to get up every morning to go out and provide for his family, how can he *not* start thinking, "She's not doing such a bad job herself"?

After looking at my own attitudes and those of many of my friends, I find we are too preoccupied with our housework, children, and ourselves to give enough thought to our most cherished "possession." We become too involved with what we don't like about our husbands and forget to remind ourselves of their good qualities.

I've heard too many women complain that their men only want them to cook and clean and do the laundry, solely for sexual satisfaction. Well, if that is true, perhaps both partners are taking each other for granted.

Try to find out what your husband thinks *you* think about him. Does he feel that you take him for granted because he will always bring home a paycheck? Does he feel that you don't appreciate his anxiety about his capabilities as your lover? (*Do* you make him feel that your sexual satisfaction is totally *his* responsibility?) Does he wonder if you are aware of his feelings of neglect when the children infringe on his time with you? (*Do* you take for granted that you will both live forever and so you will have the time to show him your appreciation and love *after* the children are gone?)

If we would live each day as though it were our last—how much we would appreciate life and all the blessings God has given us, how much we would *not* take for granted!

Part of the reason many wives take their husbands for granted is not directly their fault (though that doesn't mean they are not responsible for their actions). People change. Attitudes and expectations are changed by age and awareness. Society changes. The twenty-one-year-old man you married was just starting out in adult life. Perhaps he was still finishing his schooling. But each year is a step upward toward maturity. Ideally, he rose in his chosen profession. Then your husband became a father, and he had to learn to set good examples. So he adapted, he changed. But what about you, his wife? Have you learned new ways to give him the added comfort, respect, and admiration he is entitled to for his achievements?

As time goes by, many women become so totally involved with the concerns of the home, putting them before anything else, that they lose sight of their mates' struggle to provide for them and at the same time grow and mature. Appreciating your man, who is making your home life possible—not taking him for granted—will go a long way toward satisfying his basic human needs. He must feel emotionally important to another person—*you!*

Take some time for a little self-examination. For instance, what attracted your husband to you in the first place? Are you still the same person he married? Did you fantasize that he was the *perfect* man? It's not a role he (or anyone) can live up to. People don't always marry for the "right" reasons. Sometimes it is to escape from unhappy circumstances, or for the status that marriage provides. Both reasons easily lead to taking the partner for granted.

Try not to assume that your husband will do the same things for you that your father did for *his* wife. There were times when I became frustrated because my husband could not do something around the house that I had seen my father do. But now I have learned to stop myself and say "Oleda, you didn't marry your father. You married Steve, a very special man who can do things that your father couldn't. He's not your father, he's your husband. And you are not his daughter, you're his wife."

Taking your husband for granted with regard to the children can cause a problem in either of two ways. If you make a major decision about the children before consulting him, for instance, you are taking for granted that he will agree with you, thus usurping his place as head of the family in your children's eyes. On the other hand, if you make him totally responsible for *all* decisions, you are making him appear more authoritative than he is or wishes to be—and you are also placing additional pressures on him if he has to come home from the jungle and face still another multitude of decisions.

I never remember my mother hitting my father with a basketful of problems the minute he walked in the door. What she did was very subtle. At dinner she'd say, "I'm having trouble with the washer again, and I don't think I'll use plumber X again. But I'm not sure about plumber Y, either. Who do you think would be better at the job?"

In this way my father was being appealed to as an authority—but for an opinion, not a decision. Consequently, he could consider the situation calmly.

A lot of us take the money our husbands earn for granted. Many husbands like to have control over their money, and some wives may find it difficult to accept the fact that they are dependent on whatever their husbands choose to give them. If you have this problem, remember that your husband may have found it difficult to realize that his income was no longer all his, that he must share it with his entire family. If he holds back, more than likely it is not a criticism of you. He is probably doing what his father did with his mother. Or perhaps he believes that managing financial affairs is a masculine duty. There are ways of showing him that you can help manage the money. You probably get a certain amount for groceries and incidentals. If he can be shown that you are not extravagant and spend the money wisely, he is more likely to work out an agreeable compromise. Once he sees that you can handle this part of your relationship, he will very likely relax and indulge you more.

Consideration, courtesy, and respect will go a long way in preventing you from taking your husband for granted. In return, it will be impossible for him to take you for granted. Affection and appreciation will be your reward.

## What You Can Learn From Your Marvelous Man

Some of the characteristics that men have are instinctive, God-given qualities that define them as men. They are good qualities, ones that attract women to men in the first place. Women are not born with these qualities, although they can learn to acquire them. But by highlighting these "special" qualities of men, I don't mean to minimize women's particular talents.

*Men See the Forest Instead of the Trees.* Men are very good at seeing a problem from a broad point of view. Women become bogged down by each little detail. Since men are more likely to see the end result first, they can cut through all the step-by-step hassle. They see the overall picture.

I'm not saying that seeing the trees is less important than seeing the forest. Both are necessary. But if you could fly like a bird and look down on the *entire* situation, you might be able to solve your problems with more ease. If you can learn this from your husband, you may be able to prevent conflicts and save time.

*A Man's Job Is Only Part of His Life.* Your job, homemaking, seems to take up most of your time—it would be nice if there were more than twenty-four hours in a day. Perhaps you could gain more time through better organization. Then you would be free to fulfill other needs in your life. (For instance, allot certain hours each day for housework and the rest of the time for a new activity.) The more you fulfill

26

yourself through activities that interest you, the more interesting *you* will be.

Your husband works hard at his job, but he does understand that there is a time to relax and do other things. If you plan it right, it can work that way for you, too.

*Men Are More Willing to Tackle the Odds.* They have a sense of adventure and they look forward to challenges. And they are confident in their ability to accept challenges. They are willing to tackle the odds because they don't get bogged down with all the little steps along the way. They see the end result and work backward with the goal always in mind. Another good lesson from our marvelous men.

*Men Love to Consume Information on Many Subjects.* Men know this about themselves, and so they just naturally get together whenever they want to talk about the economy, politics, or any other broad subject.

A woman's mind is just as good as a man's, but the daily consumption of information just isn't a habit for her, as it is for a man. If you read the newspaper each day, you will know what is happening in the world—and the next time your husband talks about foreign affairs, politics, or the average whatever, you can join in. Before long, he will come to *you* looking for a conversation.

If he has stocks, follow them; know if they are up or down, whether they pay dividends and how much. Try to find out why a particular stock has dropped.

Keeping up with the bank interest rates is also interesting, because it is an indication of how our economy is going. It probably affects you personally, too. Know also what interest rate you are getting on your savings. It's fun to know these facts, and even more fun to analyze them.

If you find subjects that interest you deeply, discuss them with your husband, ask his opinion. Talking about things other than yourself, home, and children will encourage him to talk to you more.

Here is my routine for "keeping up with my man":

*Each day*

Read a good newspaper, one that is not totally gossip-oriented and covers the world situation. Spend fifteen to thirty minutes. Try to read through the *entire* newspaper, even if it means skimming sometimes.

Listen to the news on radio and TV. If you don't have the extra time, listen while you are cleaning, cooking, or dressing. (The radio usually says it faster and more precisely.)

*Each week*

Read leisurely for information. I find *Time* or *Newsweek* the best. These magazines give a good, over-all view of what's going on in the world.

Now draw your own conclusions from what you have read. You are analyzing what the top journalists in the country have to say about business, law, medicine, art, environment, religion, and one of your man's favorite subjects—sports. You'll be ready to give your husband's male friends a little conversation, and soon *you* will be sought after for your opinion by your husband. He will also be proud of your interest.

If you are having guests for dinner, let "what happened to the kids at school today" wait until you are alone with him, and talk about subjects everyone can share.

*Monthly*

Read periodicals that can add to your information. Consume information on subjects you can talk over with your husband. Of course, it is a good idea to keep up with beauty and fashion, but these subjects aren't interesting to him. Also buy books on the subjects you want to become more familiar with—and don't forget the library.

## Your Man's Work: Where Do You Fit In?

How a man does at his work indicates to him how he is doing in life. His work takes up a very large part of his planning, thinking, and hoping. But that doesn't mean you and the children aren't important to him. It is simply that women were created to be nurturers, to concentrate on their families; men were made to look outward—have wider horizons.

A man's work tells him how he should measure himself and how others measure him, including his wife and family. Without a good public self-image, he may be difficult to live with. His mood is governed by unpleasant changes in his work routine, by someone else's getting the promotion he was hoping for, by an impossible deadline he must meet, a job change he is considering, and so on.

From birth, a man is programmed to work the rest of his life, so it is to be expected that his satisfaction will lie in the success he can attain through his work. If you can just remember how natural it is for your husband to feel this way about his work, it will help you in coping with whatever stress he is under and will minimize yours. Don't let a difficult time for him hurt your relationship. Keep the situation in perspective—he's got a problem outside the home, not with you, and anyway it will probably be *short-lived.*

He may very well bring his problem home—hope that he does—and it's up to you to support him emotionally and psychologically during this time. Make sure he is seeing his problem in proper perspective. He does so well with your problems, but now that he has one of his own, the situation can seem overwhelming and grow out of proportion. He must know that he is not alone.

Prevent him from feeling humiliated or depressed. You can do this partly by trying to encourage him to talk about his future, and about how to *solve* the situation—discourage him from going on and on about "how it happened" or "who was at fault." This must be done very subtly or he will think you are not interested in what he's saying. Asking him a question about his next move will get him out of feeling sorry for himself and start him thinking constructively. Above all, listen to him, hold his hand, keep repeating how much you love him and admire him.

Where do you fit in when your husband's work is satisfactory or progressing well? He then considers his family his "fun time"—time to relax from his *real* work—even it includes his helping you solve your problems or the children do their homework.

You will do well to remember how *he* sees *you.* Forget what women's liberation says; he needs you and will always need you for his lighter side of life. What's so wrong with that! I find it very satisfying and rewarding to be considered the fun part of my husband's life.

## Sharing Your Husband's Leisure

Tremendous pleasure can come from sharing leisure with your husband. It's the enthusiasm that makes it so enjoyable. What suits one couple will not suit another; so find out what your husband enjoys and learn about it so you can share it together.

My husband and I are equally enthusiastic about TV documentaries on almost any subject. When he or I find one listed in *TV Guide,* we can't wait to tell each other. We know it will bring a source of enjoyment to both of us. Then we work out our schedule so that we can relax together when the show is on.

My friends Marilyn and Harold spend their leisure-time playing tennis together. My sister, Francey, and her husband love to entertain in their home. My friends Johnnie and Matthew love to play golf together and then have lunch, when they gloat over their terrific shots and analyze the lousy ones.

A couple can read together, take a walk together, collect stamps or coins, play bridge, exercise, plant a garden, fish—or just sit together watching the sunset. These are just a few suggestions. It doesn't matter what you do as long as it's something you *both* want to do and like to talk about.

If your husband spends his leisure time doing something that you have no interest in, don't put it down or complain. Instead, learn to enjoy what he enjoys. Once you investigate and make an effort, you might find that you are as enthusiastic as he is. How much more he will appreciate you if you play tennis with him, or bowl, or golf, or watch football games on TV than if you pout and turn to your own activities.

Maybe you don't always want to do what he wants

31

to, but try. If you make an effort to accommodate him you will be rewarded: a husband who knows a wife is with him all the way will be much more considerate and kind. And it works both ways. Watch, and I bet he'll surprise you one day by suggesting that you both do something he knows you especially like.

## The "Run-away" Husband

I feel a responsibility to pass on some unhappy information I gained through my research for this book. It's not pleasant to read, but it must be faced. To know about possible dangers is the first step toward preparing yourself to fight them.

More and more husbands are "running away" from home—an estimated two hundred thousand in the U.S. every year. We must ask ourselves two questions: Why do they leave? What can we do to prevent it?

A husband most often leaves home because of stress in the marital relationship. He has reached *his* breaking point and he feels he cannot stand it any longer. He has two options. He can ride out the storm and seek the help of a third party, such as a marriage counselor, or he can escape, run away.

What brings a man to this point of no return is a *failure to communicate*. Wife and husband have stopped really talking to each other. Was the woman too busy with herself, the house, the children, and her friends to see her own husband's tension building up? Many times the wife had no idea her husband planned to disappear. He just up and left, and *then* she thinks back—"Well, maybe he did seem a little uptight, like he had something he wanted to tell me."

The communication lines must stay open. That way

tension does not have time to build up. Encourage your husband to talk about what is bothering him, and then try to discover what can be done to ease some of the pressure. It doesn't matter if some stress is caused by his own doing; it is still up to you to help him out of it.

If he is a gambler, for instance, and he builds up a large debt, it will be difficult for him to confess this to you. And if he has spent all the family's savings to pay it, he will be so embarrassed that he might think his only choice is to disappear.

For men who are vulnerable to this kind of stress or reaction, an understanding wife is essential. Keep assuring him that you love him, that you still admire him and have faith in his ability to work out the problem with God's help. A time of stress is a good time to join together in prayer.

Infidelity is one of the major stress points. The way you handle the situation—assuming you want to keep your husband—is crucial; it can make or break the marriage. If this extramarital affair is only an affair and is *his* secret, the chances are the marriage can remain intact. Now I'm not advising a woman to remain silent about her husband's love affairs. My own reaction to the situation, if it should happen to me, would be to talk to my husband through those open communication lines and try to find out what made him go that route. I would also consult my minister for guidance, and I would pray. Then I would try to correct whatever failing I had that sent my husband to another woman.

Husbands run away from nagging wives, from wives who add to their burdens and create tension at the day's end, from wives who berate them and demean them—in other words, from wives who aren't loving, comforting, and reassuring. Wives who are

33

true wives as God meant them to be don't lose their husbands. A true wife understands her husband and helps him. She never allows herself to become a hindrance or a burden.

If a woman loves her man and wants to keep him, she must be able to communicate. To be able to communicate she must always keep the lines open by showing a willingness to listen and an assurance that she is "with him." Encourage him to confide in you. If he knows you are on his side, he will learn to bare his fears and disillusionments to you without fear of rejection. You will understand him better and he will love you more for it. If you can accomplish this, you are well on the way to a solid relationship.

## Don't Let Your Husband's Job Leave You Behind

If your husband gets a promotion, make sure you find out what's expected of *him;* then you will know what is expected of you. A wife can be either a great drawback or a great asset to her husband in his new job. A wife can be a drawback if she doesn't really know the extent of her influence in relation to her husband's job. Many a man has been considered for an important position only to be passed over because his wife was regarded as a liability.

If you are to be an asset, then you must accept the fact that more is expected of you. You will gain great satisfaction from knowing that you have kept pace with your husband. And think how proud he will be of *you.* Remember that while your husband's job is important to him as a job, it is also what he needs to support *you* and the children.

Your husband may not even think of your part in his promotion at the beginning. So you have to take the initiative in finding out what is needed from you. Don't end up sabotaging his chances for success because of ignorance.

First of all, let him know how happy you are for him. Then ask him to sit down and talk over his new plans and how you can fit in and help out. Let him know you are on his team and that you want to move forward *with* him. This means you should present yourself to your best advantage.

With your husband's approval, you might invite his boss and his wife over for dinner or a Sunday afternoon luncheon. If you have any fears about the success of your meal, solve them on your own. Ask a good cook, or take a few quick lessons, or test a few recipes before the big day. Don't practice on the boss and his wife! And remember not to be too formal. Relax, be at ease and act natural. But let your husband know he can depend on you.

In my husband's business, it's necessary that we have business parties once in a while. The first time, I was so nervous I was shaking. How could *I* decide what food to serve? How much food should I have? It was winter—how could I handle coats for seventy-five people? Where would I rent all those dishes? How much liquor and what kind? Without giving all these worries to Steve, I went to my Amy Vanderbilt etiquette book. She told me a lot. Then I phoned my friend Marilyn, who had been through this many times with her husband. She advised me and also gave me a list of rental companies for glasses, dishes, coat racks, et cetera. My husband didn't think very much about getting that party together. But he did think a lot about it *afterward* and he told me how pleased he was. Now I feel very comfortable preparing for his business-social gatherings.

It's not only the food preparation you must be

aware of. You should also consider carefully the way you dress for these occasions. If you appear too flamboyant, or too obviously sexy, or too sloppy, it will reflect poorly on your husband. Select something simple—soft colors, basic styling (nothing too young-looking), and do not overdo the jewelry. Keep your hair style simple, too. Don't wear too much make-up or garish nail polish.

If you really want to help your husband, make sure you keep your eyes and ears open for what's going on in his type of business and read the newspaper *well* for several days before your encounter with the new acquaintances, so that you won't feel at a loss for conversation or left out.

Be polite, self-spoken, and a lady always.

With your willingness to improve yourself on behalf of your husband, he cannot help loving you more. And all good things that come to him will come to you, too.

# 3

# Making a Marriage Work

## Lover and Friend

WHEN I WAS a child, I thought that loving was the
same as liking, only much stronger. For many years
it was a puzzle to me. As I grew older, I decided
that it was necessary to like someone you love, but
it was not necessary to love someone you like.

Loving and liking do have many similarities. But
they affect your relationship with your husband in
different ways. Loving is on a more subconscious
level; liking is on a more conscious level. It's easier
to love, because it's not something you *do*—it just
"happens." Liking is related more with the real world
and with your husband as he really is—the person he
is. You like your husband because he is nice. He
brings you pleasure and happiness. You can share
with him. And he is a good person.

If you only *love,* your relationship will be deep
and emotional, but very possibly often unpleasant.
If you only *like,* your relationship will be pleasant
enough, but shallow and vulnerable emotionally. In
order to have a great marriage, *you must achieve
both loving and liking with your husband*.

To me, loving is like preparing a gourmet banquet.

Every ingredient must be just right. You have to balance the spices exactly and taste and test until you have perfect results. Love is not only that churning feeling you have in the pit of your stomach every time your man walks into a room. To this feeling you add a sense of belonging and the ability to identify yourself with this man and no other.

You want to share everything possible with your husband, to be a part of him. You tingle when he touches you. Only he can satisfy your sexual needs, and you his. His desires come before yours because your happiness depends on pleasing him. And there is a sense of commitment, of being bound together with him in the sight of God and man. Yes, there is a sense of being blessed . . . of the rightness of your union.

But love is not enough. It's like making a fancy French recipe and leaving out just that dash of wine that gives it its body. Liking is the wine in marriage. You have got to like your man, share his interests, have fun with him . . . enjoy, laugh, joke and kid. *Be friends.*

When you like your husband, it is much easier to express your thoughts and opinions to him. Don't feel shy about saying "I like your smile," or "You have good legs," or "I like the way you dance," or "It's fun doing things with you."

Love is not as easy to express, because it means showing your *feelings.* Sometimes you will feel like a block of ice that will have to melt before you can truly say what you feel. But there are other ways to express your feelings. Worrying about your husband is an indirect way of saying I love you. Simply *wanting* to be with him is also an expression of love.

Loving and liking your husband must go together for a real marriage.

## *Making His Love Last*

In the early years of marriage, the romantic side of love and sexual desire are dominant. The longer you live together, the more a genuine liking becomes important in cementing the relationship. This does not mean that you fall out of love; just that the infatuation has been replaced by a more secure and realistic long-range love. Kindness, consideration, loyalty, admiration, sympathy, and respect are the most important qualities for a life-long relationship.

Teen-agers talk about love all the time. Fifteen-year-olds fall in love with each other, with movie stars, rock singers, sports heroes. Each week brings a new "love." This isn't love; this is infatuation. Oh, don't we all remember this time well! The pains! The agony! The feeling that you'll never survive!

Unfortunately, some adults never make the transition from infatuation to love. Too often, supposedly mature people marry and divorce, remarry and re-divorce. "Till death do us part" doesn't seem to have much meaning in the world today.

But, if you understand what true love is and approach the marital situation as a grown-up instead of as a teen-ager moony-eyed over Robert Redford or Paul Newman, you can build a solid, secure relationship.

First of all, love should be a part of your marriage on every level—emotional, psychological, spiritual, physical.

Love is not something to be used only as needed. Love is not hearts and flowers. Love is not a game. Love between two adults is serious business. There are several aspects to love:

*Emotional love*—giving warmth and understanding to his joys, sorrows, fears, and hates.

*Psychological love*—being aware of his feelings and motivations and accepting them graciously.

*Spiritual love*—loving him as God meant you to, according to His scriptures.

*Physical love*—expressing your love through your physical efforts to satisfy his needs.

Deep, mature love encompasses all of these. A lasting love does not "just happen." It takes a lot of effort and willingness to give. Attaining such a love is the greatest reward of life.

## The Power of Your Love

The highest expression of love's potency is your unadulterated ability to give willingly to your husband. There are many things you couldn't do with a full heart if you did not love him. You couldn't respond to his physical and emotional needs. You couldn't give to him what is alive in you. You couldn't share his joys, knowledge, interests, and sadness.

Love teaches you to interpret the events of your life from the viewpoint of your husband. For example: I keep house for the man I love, not just as a necessity for myself. Love has given me the insight to be more tolerant and understanding of my husband. Without it, I might complain every time I find Steve's shoes in the middle of the bedroom floor, instead of just putting them away with love. The act of giving enables you to experience the deepest form of your inner resources.

Love is something without which we cannot truly live; we seek to experience love out of a deep need to form a close relationship with someone. "To love and be loved." Your husband is that person.

Love can inspire you and your husband to do your best work. It helps you release one another's potential. It gives you confidence in your personality. It increases your ability to cope with people in general —in short, love enriches your life.

## Laughter

My husband and I have an argument and then there is a cold silence. Steve stares at me angrily and I glare at him. He looks so funny to me when he is mad that I soon begin to smile and the smile turns into a burst of laughter from both of us. We realize the argument was dumb in the first place. Our wounds have been healed.

Laughter, like crying, represents a necessary discharge of emotional energy. Being able to laugh with your husband after a disagreement has created a flare-up can heal the rift. I remember the time I was so mad at Steve I could have cut off all his trousers to short pants. I *had* to think of a way to release my anger and make my point without doing permanent damage to our relationship. Then I got an idea. I sent a card to his office. On the outside it read "I was thinking of you." Inside was a small, clear-plastic bag with little bits of garbage in it. He thought it was so funny, he brought some flowers home in exchange for the garbage. We both laughed!

God reminds us that we must learn to handle our tempers. "A soft answer turneth away wrath." A soft answer or laughter—how much better these are than voices screaming abuse. A husband and a wife yelling at one another in a TV comedy can be funny. But if it's you and your husband at home, it's not comedy; it's tragedy.

Laughter plays a big part in any relationship but it

is an essential ingredient for a successful marriage. It reassures him that he is accepted. If you can see humor in a particular predicament, it will help reduce the tension and allow you some measure of control over the circumstances.

As long as you are not laughting *at* him, it will increase bonds of affection and deeply enhance your relationship. And your life will be a great deal easier, and your relationship will be less hurtful, if you follow the gentle approach.

When my son David was born, I eagerly waited for his first smile. No doctor or nurse could tell me that his smile might mean he had a tummy ache! I knew his smile meant that he loved me and that there was something between us—that special something between mother and child.

Humor is also important in dealing with children. For instance, one day, I got into an argument with my son. I don't even remember what it was about except that it was the usual replay you have with a preadolescent. All of a sudden, I lost my temper and shouted at him: "That's it! No more TV, ever!" And even as I was shouting, I seemed to be hearing an echo. It came to me that every time David and I had a fight, I ended up with the same dreary threat— no TV. And I began to laugh. At first David was annoyed and demanded to know why I was laughing. Through my giggles I said: "Because I always say that." And as we both saw the humor of my predictable pattern, we both broke down and roared. Needless to say, our argument came to an abrupt and amiable halt.

Laughing at yourself can help heal a crisis. It also helps keep a problem in perspective and ensures a much more comfortable, loving relationship with both your husband and your children.

Ella Wheeler Wilcox was a nineteenth-century poet, journalist—and homemaker. Of all her writings, these perceptive words are perhaps the most famous: "Laugh, and the world laughs with you; Weep, and you weep alone."

## The Value of Tenderness

Tenderness is a necessary part of an intimate relationship; it means being aware of and sensitive to your husband, anticipating and responding to his moods. Tenderness is in your voice and in your touch, in the way you take care of your husband's needs. For instance, I always fluff Steve's pillow before he gets in bed at night. That's just a little something to show him I care. And I enjoy caring.

If tenderness is absent from your relationship with your husband, it can increase his sense of insecurity. Tenderness makes him feel warm and wanted.

Your husband may find it difficult to be tender, even though he loves you very much. This is due to his upbringing and his male instincts. He may feel that tenderness is strictly a feminine quality. Not *all* men feel this way, but most do. He may want to be tender but cannot out of embarrassment or a feeling that it would be unmanly.

How can you bring him around? It isn't easy, but once you do it's worth all the effort.

When your husband shows even the slightest tenderness, let him know that you admire him more for it. Bring him a cup of coffee, a surprise gift, or make a special dinner for him. If you respond soon after his display of tenderness with a kiss, a touch, or a kind word, it will encourage him to "let go" again. But do have patience. Displaying tenderness comes very hard for many men.

When he realizes that you appreciate his displays of tenderness and that his masculinity has not been threatened, he will overcome his hesitation.

## Showing Your Affection

Affection is one of the easiest and most enjoyable ways to express love to your husband. With a little imagination, you can show affection every day.

Anything you do for him with love is showing affection. Touching him at *any* time, for no reason at all, is showing affection. Leaving a note on his pillow or on his desk is showing affection.

Many times when Steve travels, I pack his bag. Often he will find a note from me when he unpacks later, reminding him that I love him. When I bring him a cup of coffee while he's working at home, that's affection. Mailing a card to him when he is away on even at his office is showing affection.

Affection is contagious—if you do it long enough, he will soon be more affectionate to you.

## Trust Strengthens Your Relationship

Deep, firm trust is a slow process. It doesn't happen overnight. But once you and your partner have sufficient trust in one another, negative feelings can be expressed and discussed amiably. Each discussion the two of you have will mark a growing point in your relationship and further reinforce your mutual trust.

Trust helps to weather times of loneliness, illness, feelings of inadequacy, and even financial difficulties. Trust is based on honesty. The trust between my husband and me was earned by mutual openness and frankness. We share our secrets, yet we never encroach on each other's privacy. The sharing of secrets doesn't mean prying.

Steve and I become aware of each other's feelings and desires because we discuss them. There is no chance for resentment or suspicion to build up. Time has proven our sincerity with one another. As our trust increases, our relationship matures.

## Give Your Man the Respect He Deserves

Respect provides a firm basis for a stable relationship with your husband. Respect in love goes hand in hand with security, as the Bible tells us: "Each one of you must love his wife as he loves himself; and let every wife respect her husband."

If you carry this attitude into everyday life, your marriage will flourish. But you must be aware of both your husband *and* yourself, and of the rights you have as individuals. Respect sets limits on the disruptive elements of your relationship. It helps untangle the emotional and sexual conflicts in your marriage and allows you to deal with his shortcomings and understand your own.

The deeper the love, the deeper the respect. This is not to say that, if we respect someone, we love them. We can respect someone (a politician, for instance) and not even like him. But respect is necessary for a lasting love. You show your respect for your husband when you speak well of him to other people outside your home. Also by the way you act with your husband in public. If you turn your back to him while you talk to someone else, it shows you do not respect him enough to include him in the conversation.

When I talk to friends—new or old—my respect for my husband will be evaluated by how and what I say about him. If I refer to him as "my old man," belittle him, be contemptuous of him, or show a ho-hum attitude, I will lower respect not only for him but also for myself. My friends cannot respect me if I insult my husband in public. If you have enough *self-respect*, you will not need to try to destroy your husband's image in public.

Mutual respect provides a sound basis for a secure, loving marriage; the more respect you give to your husband, the more respect he'll give to you.

## Privacy in Marriage: How Much Do We Need?

Privacy is necessary for everyone, but the amount varies according to the individual's personality. Some people seem to want to live their lives in a crowd. Others are shy and bloom quietly in peaceful, serene surroundings. But we all need moments of "aloneness," time to consult with our inner selves. I know that I am buoyed up and rejuvenated if I can snatch fifteen minutes in a church. Alone in a pew, without others, without a service going on, I can listen to myself and I can talk to God.

Today, we hear a great deal about "togetherness" —and that's great. We should be together with our husbands and families—that, after all, is what life is about. But I am so much more able to be "together" with my loved ones if I can occasionally have a few moments of "aloneness."

When you marry, you are told by the Bible that you are united by God as "one." But God did not mean that you had to know *everything* your partner was thinking and doing. You are *two* people living *two* lives together. Living *one* life shared by *two* can strip the other totally of his privacy.

What is privacy? For some people it is just being allowed personal freedoms such as phone calls, mail, new friends, a talk with another member of the family, without being pestered with "who, what, when, where, and how." If you *must* know *everything* your husband is thinking or doing, you are not giving him the necessary privacy he needs. Encourage him to take a quiet nap when he comes home from work, or to read a magazine, take a walk alone, or get involved in his hobby alone.

Ideally, you have worked out your schedule during the day so that you, too, can have some privacy. Your "aloneness" time will not only keep you fresh for the moments you and he share; it will also allow you to be fresh just for *him*.

I often think that Steve has less privacy than I do. He works in an office where there is very little privacy. He has to stay on his toes *all the time*. He goes through this every working day, all his life. For this reason, I make sure that Steve has some time alone with no interruptions. It gives him an opportunity to unwind and get himself together so that *we* can be together.

Your children, too, need privacy to discover themselves. As the home organizer, you can instill in your children the realization that *everyone* needs privacy. Schedule "aloneness" for your husband when he comes home, for the children after they do their homework, and for yourself when you feel you need a moment of seclusion. You should make your children understand that seeking privacy is not an expression of rejection, but a necessary time to keep in touch with oneself.

My son was taught partial independence at an early age. He learned to amuse himself occasionally, and to be alone in his room at times.

I remember one very funny incident when he was about five. In the midst of a game we had been playing, he got up and said, "That's enough, Mom."

"Don't you want to play any more?" I asked, rather surprised. "No, thanks," he said and walked toward his room. "I though we were having a good time," I said, perplexed. "We were, Mom. But now I'd like some privacy." Well, it took me back for a moment, but then I realized he was repeating to me what he had heard me say many times. I am quite proud of myself that from a very early age David valued privacy, both for himself and others.

I don't believe in everything being discussed in front of the children. Private discussions are often necessary between parents and other adults. Personal conversations about people, sex, or other problems should be discussed away from the ears of the young ones. Children should be politely asked to amuse themselves elsewhere.

Children seem to be born nosy. How often have I heard from other mothers that the moment they pick up a telephone receiver to make a call a child appears like magic. When I have a telephone call and I feel my son should not have the liberty of hearing what is said, all I have to tell him is, "David, it's a private call—would you mind?" Of course, he is afforded the same courtesy. I never feel guilty about doing this, because it teaches my son to respect other people's privacy and to respect his own. It also teaches him to learn to do things on his own, to be more self-reliant, and he is.

Are you giving your husband the privacy he deserves?

• Ask your husband if he would like some privacy right now.

• Give him privacy while on the phone as you would for a guest. Don't ask who it was after every phone call.

• *Never* open any of his mail.

● Make sure he has *some* time each day alone to do what he pleases.
● No trespassing on your husband's personal property.
● Feed the children early once in a while so you and your husband can eat alone.

In addition to having side interests of my own, I personally need ten to fifteen minutes of "aloneness" each day to lean my head back in a chair, prop up my feet, and just think. My mind is free to go wherever it wants. I follow it and delve into every possibility on the subjects it takes me to. It's really time well spent. I may think about a special dinner for my husband, or plan an evening of fun in the bedroom for both of us, or plan my week's assignments. Sometimes I make a list of people I should phone or write. The quietness of privacy gives me the opportunity to think of things I may never have thought of without it.

## Keep Talking

The more freely you communicate with your husband, the stronger and deeper your relationship will be. Without communication, there is no relationship. So the real issue is how to make communication as constructive and beneficial as possible.

Close relationships (how much closer can you get than in marriage) require work and renewal of interest to even survive, much less to grow and be enriched.

After a few years of marriage, it's quite possible to settle down to a routine that involves little *real* communication. Communication can begin to backfire or to create trouble. A reminder begins to sound like nagging. A suggestion begins to sound like controlling. An offer of help begins to sound like "I don't think you're capable of doing it." For example, if your husband is cleaning the garage floor and you object to the way he is doing it, you might say "Here, let *me* do it." This automatically tells him you think he's doing a lousy job. But if you say, gently, "Honey, I desperately need you to help David with his homework. I'll finish this for you," you have solved the situation tactfully.

In spite of the fact that wives have all the modern conveniences, which give them more time for themselves than their sisters of yesteryear had, husbands often come home to a reception of boredom and irritability. Some women don't care how or when they express their tensions. That's unfair.

In marriage (because of the depth of the relationship and because of continued closeness) tension can prevent communication; if the tension is too great between you and your husband, it might cause you to pour out your feelings too emotionally or else to clam up completely.

Tension releasing by way of communication is not always that simple. Often quarrels can't be avoided, no matter how hard you try. The couple that *never* quarrels may not care enough. Quarrels can clear the air and the aftermath *can* be a wonderful reunion. But if these sparring matches are not resolved each time and put out of mind, then resentment is kept alive, and even builds up. Forget it; don't be an elephant. Once the fight's over, that should be the end of it. Don't go throwing up the past to him or you just might not have a future.

How do you open these lines of communication? Communication *can* be cultivated. Talking, while only one of the ways to communicate with your husband, is perhaps the best. A continuous effort to discuss what is being experienced in your relationship and life only enriches your marriage. Every day, before

Steve comes home, I run through a list of subjects I want to talk over with him that night. If he's not interested in an item on my list, I drop it; but I'm never at a loss for words.

Another way is to ask your husband to tell you when he has time to sit down with you and talk. Tell him you realize that there's tension and say, "Let's find out what's at the bottom of it." Be willing to *listen* as much as talk. If you know what he is feeling, you can help relieve the tension. Just the fact that you care enough to ask will begin to relieve the tension.

Whatever kind of communication takes place the first five minutes after my husband comes home sets the pace for the rest of the evening. I communicate with my husband when I touch him. A kiss when he comes through the door tells him I care about him and am happy to see him home. A touch on his shoulder as I pass his chair means I know he is there—I care. If I stroke his hand when I talk to him, it says I care. If I straighten his hair or tie, it tells him I care. Touching—sharing warmth and understanding—should be an *every*day form of communication. The littlest gesture can display love and reassurance, relieve tension and anxieties, without your saying one word.

Sometimes, though, just using a word like "sweetheart," "dear," "love," "darling" will communicate to your husband that he *is* special to you.

What you should avoid if you hope to keep the lines of communication open: saying things like "I can do it better" and "I could have done it faster," insincerity, compulsive talking, constantly interrupting, nonstop unloading of personal problems, being a poor listener, lecturing, being opinionated, disapproving of everything, and constantly contradicting.

Beware of talking *too* much. Also, what subjects are

you talking about? If you are too anxious to get your husband to talk, you may be talking for him.

One stopper of communication is the overanxious habit of finishing your husband's sentences or breaking into the conversation before he finishes talking. You feel so sure that you know what he is going to say and want so much for him to know that you are following his train of thought—that's fine. But don't cut him off. This can lead to misunderstanding, because you don't actually hear what he means and he, in turn, feels that you don't *want* to hear what *he* is saying. So, if you are lucky enough to have a husband who is still talking to you, *listen* to what he is saying and let him finish before you speak. It's a politeness you give to others—why not to your husband, above all?

Another deterrent of communication *and* love is the inability to say I'm sorry. Your pride gets in the way or you honestly feel it was not your fault. But continually insisting you are in the right *all* the time implies that you are perfect and sitting in judgment of your husband, who is *always* wrong. Think how he must feel! Put yourself in his place. Would you feel confident and loving toward someone who is always putting you down? Saying, in a sense, I'm better than you or I know more than you do can destroy love. That's what is called castration.

If you can say, "I'm sorry," or indicate in some way that you realize you were mistaken, your attitude will change, and so will his. If you are obviously understanding he will open up without fear of being rebuffed.

When you realize that there are two sides to every story or that your husband might have a different view of a situation, you will automatically become more understanding and easier to talk to. So try saying

"I'm sorry" once in a while. You'll find, even if he doesn't show it immediately, that whatever barriers there are will gradually drop. He will eventually start talking to you again and begin to enjoy your company more.

## Talking as a Pastime

One of my favorite pleasures is talking with my husband. I actually plan it as a pastime. When I know he is not pressed for time in the evening, I will set the table with a flower or candles and wine. I will choose a couple of current subjects that are of interest to both of us, and start out by asking *his* opinion. He always has one, *given the chance*. Sometimes we are at the table for two hours.

If your husband has not really communicated for many years, you must have patience. Almost all husbands can become communicative—it's a matter of studying first your communicative habits and then his.

A good way to start getting him to talk is when there are other people around, even your children (if they are old enough to carry on a conversation). For example, not so long ago Steve and I went skiing. We met a man who was such a fantastic skier that he almost danced on the slopes. A short time afterward we were having dinner with a couple who sometimes ski with us. I began to tell them about this exceptional skier and I said to Steve, "You explain his ability— you can do it so well." And he *did* explain it. Steve has no problem whatsoever with "something to say," but if I overpowered him with too much talk, he would be a "talk-to-me" problem.

One effective and easy way to get communication flowing is to lend a sympathetic ear to your husband. Stop whatever you are doing if he shows the slightest inclination to talk. Give him a sympathetic, concerned glance—and listen.

When you do talk, think carefully about what you want to say. Try to choose subjects *other* than your household problems, what the kids did wrong, or all your aches and pains. Try to relax him with conversation, not distress him. Make sure you are not talking about the same subject too often, especially if it is something he is not very interested in. It will take time, so don't expect to see a big change in a few days. After all, he's been conditioned for years.

Listen to his complaints and repeat them so that you thoroughly understand. Then, don't argue, but discuss the problems rationally. Help him to know that you are sympathetic.

Let him get his complaints out of his system. This, too, will open up communication between you. When Steve complains about a fast deadline on a project, he says, "My client has given me an impossible deadline to meet." Now, I could say, "Everyone has their problems. I had my share today, too. I'm sure the client wouldn't ask for the impossible." That's negative. What I should say is, "The client gave you an impossible deadline? What will you do now?" Now he knows I care about *him*.

Time planned alone, without children or friends, is very conducive to conversation. Tell him you need and like to be alone with him. Make an appointment or a date with him. How can he refuse! It's up to you, though, to see that he enjoys this time with you, that you remember all the rules of getting him to open up. If he enjoys the first date or two, it will become a natural part of your life and you'll become better friends.

Communication is providing information, exchanging ideas, re-examining goals, planning activities, sharing frustrations, fears, hopes, and opinions. It is sharing with warmth and sincerity.

In order to enable your husband to open-up and to keep the lines of communication from getting clogged, here are a few rules to follow:

1. *Don't* repeat the *same* statement *every* day when your husband leaves for and returns from work. "Have a good day, dear" can become boring if it's said every single morning at 8:15 And "How was your day, dear?" upon his return can be equally boring. Change—change—change is an excellent rule to remember.

2. Talk about *his* special interest or hobbies. Read up on whatever it is so you can offer something new to him. Ask a question about his interests or hobbies. He won't be able to resist answering.

3. Once he opens up, *listen . . . with your heart.* Respond enthusiastically and sincerely. Even repeat back a small part of what he said so he *knows* you are really listening.

4. Don't be impatient while he's talking just to have "your turn" to talk. Let him breathe between sentences. Offer concern, sincerity, and warmth in response, not competition.

5. Read up on a new subject that may interest him, then open up with "I read today that. . . . What do *you* think about it?" Widening your interests can open up more interesting conversations with him.

6. Make your husband *shine.* Tell him how great he is. He is the best husband in the world because he's yours, so let him know it.

7. Ask for his advice. You'll be telling him that you respect his knowledge and judgment.

8. When you talk don't make a short story long. Stick to the point. Men have no patience with people who ramble on and relate so many irrelevant details

that they lose sight of what they want to say. If you are this type of talker, your husband will tune you out.

9. If an argument took place and you were wrong, admit it. Say, "I was wrong" or "You were right." He will respect you for owning up to it.

Communication is important to encourage and maintain. If you do not talk to your husband and let him talk to you, the relationship cannot grow.

## *Your Maturity and Your Husband*

When I was a child, I heard "That's not very mature" from my parents many times. To me then, it meant I did not act "very grown up" about a given situation. Now I am "grown up," but I see that grown-ups do not always act mature.

What is maturity and how does it affect your relationship with your husband? Maturity is having a controlled emotional reaction to everything, a tolerant attitude at all times. It's self-reliance within your relationship. It's facing the truth about yourself and facing up to the realities of everyday life.

If you do not have a mature attitude, you will become a burden to your husband, and be too dependent. Remember, you are not another child he must shelter; you are his marriage partner. Nobody likes an emotional clinging vine. Being self-sufficient *within the framework of your marriage* will give your husband more time to *enjoy* his relationship with you and more time for you to *give* to him.

I have a friend who never seems to hear anyone else's problems. She always has bigger and better ones. The simplest conversation turns into a competition. If I want to tell her about a new dress I bought, her only reaction is to tell me about her new coat.

And she does the same thing to her husband. She's an example of not doing to others as she would have them do unto her. She never seems able to put herself in the other person's shoes.

My friend is immature, and our friendship is certainly rather shaky. But she has taught me a valuable lesson: how not to be.

If you have an eye-for-an-eye relationship with your husband, then your marriage has not reached its full potential and should be worked on. Don't keep a tally sheet with one column marked "He Did" and another with "I Did." If he comes home and says, "I've had a rough day today," don't you pipe up with "Well, I had a rougher day, the kids. . . ." He then feels that you didn't hear or, worse, that you couldn't care less about him.

## Is "Manipulate" a Dirty Word?

*Webster's* defines manipulate as "treating or working with the hands, or by mechanical means, esp. with skill. To treat or manage with the intellect. . . . Also, to manage artfully or fraudulently."

The art of manipulation is very much a part of you as a female. But it depends on *how* you manipulate. If you are deceptive or manipulate to destroy, then yes, it is a dirty word. But if you manipulate with intelligence to build something fantastic like your relationship with your man, there is nothing he won't do for you.

What would a woman's life be without the love and companionship of the opposite sex? A woman has a basic need to love and be loved.

Your man is the most important person or event in your life. You know how his love and acceptance of you makes you feel as if you are something special?

Well, he likes that feeling, too, and will love the woman who gives it to him. In order for him to make your existence worthwhile, to make you feel that being a woman is the greatest thing ever, you must make him feel that he is the best thing that ever happened to you—sexually, intellectually, emotionally —day after day.

You did this *before* he married you, so why stop now? The rewards were great then, or have you forgotten? You were interested in the things he talked about, even if you had never been interested in them before. You invited him to dinner and used your best tablecloth, glasses, and dishes—with the intention of entrancing him. You had a sense of humor then and laughed at his jokes. You wore perfume to stimulate an atmosphere of romance, and always tried to look your best. You were never caught with curlers in your hair. You wore clothing that was neat and clean and appropriate. You were kind, gentle, and polite, and wouldn't think of complaining. You admired him and let him know that his presence made you happy.

You did these things spontaneously over a period of time because you wanted his love and acceptance and approval. Is that manipulation? You bet it is! And if *you* don't manipulate your man, some other woman will!

Positive manipulation is a long-range plan. Don't worry about your man—he will *love* being manipulated this way. If you feel he is not responding to your manipulation, keep trying; don't become angry and lash out. The more you try, the sooner he will get the point. How can he *not* respond to you when you have so patiently and willingly given to him?

Here are a few important examples you can try. They don't take much effort, just a little thoughtfulness and understanding. But you will see how they can get you on the right track for *positive* manipulation, and a happier life for both of you.

*Start the Day Right.* Wake up with a pleasant attitude. Give him a hug and a kiss before you get out of bed. Make his breakfast or coffee right away—the kids can wait a minute. Your man is the king and your home is his castle. He made it all possible and must fight every day to keep it. Send him off to work with a kiss and a cheery good-by. Your part of the partnership is making the home run smoothly, and that includes breakfast time.

*Don't Bug Him at the Office.* Be intelligent and efficient enough to find the right person to handle whatever problem you might run into. If you do call him, tell him you love him and were thinking of him. If he calls you, answer with a smile in your voice, even if the TV just broke or the dish washer is gurgling soapsuds all over the floor. Don't panic! He depends on your support on the homefront.

If he calls and asks you to join him for lunch, drop everything and go. Your work is more flexible than his and he's more important than your work. Even if you had planned lunch with the girls, they should understand that your man comes first. Get a babysitter if necessary. Don't miss the chance to be with him outside the home!

*Welcome Him Home with a Smile.* Tell him you're glad he's home. He's had a rough day filled with problem solving and decision making, so let him unwind in peace. Send the kids outside or to their rooms to play. Sit down and have coffee or a drink with him, let him shed office tension. Home is his retreat from the world of business. If he wants to tell you of his trials throughout the day, listen sincerely, and don't counterattack with yours or try to tell him how to run his business (unless he asks your advice). That's *his* job and he is superior at it.

*When He Suggests Going Out in the Evening or Away for a Trip, Be Ready and Willing.* Don't use the kids as an excuse or complain that you're too tired. Whatever stands in your way, work it out! Treat each invitation as a date and look your best.

*When He Wants to Bring His Friends or Business Acquaintances Home, Welcome Them.* He wants to be proud of his home and family. Don't be jealous of his time with them. It's better that he entertains them in your home than in the local bar.

*THINK POSITIVE!* If you can efficiently handle your end of the partnership (the home and children) and still be "his girl," you will reap the rewards. He will think of you as his sunshine or his port in a storm, and his love for you will grow stronger. You set the tone. The kind of relationship you *want* from him, you must *give* to him. With a little patience and a lot of love, it will work.

## Complaining: Is It Really Necessary?

We all complain—men and women. Complaining is normal, but it is not necessary. If you have a problem or a gripe, state it in such a way that your husband doesn't think you're whining. Try to communicate positively even when stating a problem. Most men are gallant and chivalrous, and are more than willing to help their women. Like Sir Walter Raleigh they feel they can smooth over any puddle that lies in your path.

Giving aid is ego-gratifying. So let your man know that you need him—whether his muscles (to open jars) or his brains (to sort out your bills)—and he will come through for you.

Sometimes I don't even realize I am complaining. I need attention and that seems to be the easiest way to get it. But the long-range penalties of that kind of attention are quite severe. Whenever I complain about *my horrible day* to my husband, I'm sorry later. If I stop to think about it, I know I'm usually doing it to get his attention.

Now I try a new approach, which is much more successful. Perhaps you should try it, too.

Think back over the last few days and try to remember the complaints you voiced versus the interesting ideas or projects you told him about. Then, for the next few days, think one second *before* saying anything to him in the morning or when he returns from work and ask yourself (if it's a complaint), "Is this complaint something he can help me with, or am I just using it for conversation?" If it's for conversation or attention, or letting off steam, then forget it and choose a subject more interesting to him.

Don't forget, your man has his share of problems at his own job. He comes home to rest, to unwind. So be careful that you don't wind him up even more. You wouldn't do this to your friends; if you did, you would certainly soon lose them.

If you communicate in the form of complaints and do it as soon as he comes home every night, he will soon feel that you are blaming him for all of your problems each day. He's not a gigantic ear for you to snivel and whine into.

You should take a tip from your man and learn a more professional approach in order to cope. Men generally see things in a broader perspective. They see the long-range effect.

I remember complaining to Steve about a parking-lot

attendant. I had stopped the car at the stop line and *he* was supposed to take over. But he asked me two different times to get back into the car and drive it up some more. He was lazy and wanted his customers to do most of his work. I became angry and was beginning to complain to my husband that the attendant should do his own work. My husband said to me, "Don't let him upset you—he's a parking-lot attendant, not an executive." My husband saw through the whole problem and weighed the situation in it's proper perspective. How stupid of me to be so emotional about it!

Men look for the *answer* almost instantly, while women have a tendency to get too emotionally involved with the problem right away. The point is to *solve* the problem, not to complain or go on and on about it.

If there really is a problem your husband may be able to help you with, don't serve it up at dinner with the lamb chops. Save it. Choose a time that is best suited for both of you. In fact, I find that telling my husband, "I need your opinion (or advice) on something, let me know when you have time to talk about it," brings the problem out of the complaint category. He then feels that I am willing to accept the problem as mine but that I need his worldly or manly advice to solve it. His ego is boosted and he doesn't feel that I am attacking him. He becomes more curious and willing to help. By waiting to discuss the situation later, I have time to calm down about the matter and can approach it on a higher, more constructive level.

So, I try to remember not to depress my husband by pouncing on him with unpleasant things. I keep firmly in mind the realization that he, too, had a full day with problems of his own. He needs a lift, not a letdown. Just a smile and a warm welcome can give him that lift and set the mood for a pleasant evening.

## *Aggression: How to Handle It With Your Husband*

Don't you sometimes feel you just want to scream at your man or throw something? Everybody does occasionally. I sure do. That's because the close and demanding embrace of marriage offers countless opportunities for indulging the aggressive impulse.

Getting mad or blowing up or slamming a door are all natural reactions to circumstances in which you feel frustrated. But you do *not* have to act like a child throwing a temper tantrum. You *can* control your behavior to some extent if you want to. You can *learn* to react differently. After all, it is part of God's plan that men and women live in harmony.

There have been many difficult points in my marriage. Often Steve and I found ourselves fighting like two bears for the last drop of honey on a maple tree. Until I tried a new approach. Depending on how mad I was, I would sit down and write either a note or a letter to him. Then I'd wait about an hour and reread it. By that time, I had cooled down enough to make the necessary point without all the insults, and often I would throw the note away or rewrite it. Steve was delighted that he didn't have to face an angry me and he answered by note in turn. It works (most of the time) for us. Somehow it is easier to deal with the written word than face the fury of tempers aflare.

Aggression is really an admission of defeat. If you lash out physically or verbally at your husband, it will only cause him humiliation and he will usually respond in kind. Nothing is solved by slamming doors or throwing things. The only tangible result that ever had for me was a shattered dining-room mirror. And don't you think I didn't worry about the seven years' bad luck, which I certainly deserved.

If you cause your man to feel guilty and at fault too often, he may begin to brood and become silent and hostile. Such passive aggression is hard to deal with.

The best way to handle your husband, if you don't like note writing, is for *you* to stay calm. When you find yourself becoming tense, *order* yourself to take measures to stay under control. Give yourself credit for being tactful and having self-control. It is necessary and normal to "have it out" in order to clear the air. But remember, no one ever wins in an argument that has turned into World War III. Each time that happens, a part of love goes out the window; eventually it will mean irreparable damage to your relationship.

No matter what the fight is about, it's never worth it. Your job is to be a help, not a hindrance—to make your man happy. So control yourself, discuss the problem when tempers have cooled. His tenderness and love are worth every effort on your part to maintain a loving relationship.

## Crisis Time

A crisis is a testing ground for your love. It is a time you can use to strengthen your love and trust for your husband. Whether it be the loss of his job, temporary impotence, severe illness, death of a loved one or close friend, or infidelity.

When Steve was in the hospital for an operation, it was a crisis—not so much because of the operation, but because his entire business depended on his ability to get the work out. He had a feeling of hope-lessness.

I knew he had this feeling, so when I visited him each day in the hospital, I brought him everything he needed to do whatever work was possible. I also brought the books and magazines he needed to keep up with his business. When he was feeling well enough, I made visiting arrangements for his clients to see him. At the same time, I asked friends to wait another week before visiting, knowing it might be too much activity.

Ordinarily, I would've had friends visit, and made business wait if Steve were in the hospital. But I knew Steve's sense of hopelessness about being away from his business was the major problem. I had to do what would give him the most peace of mind.

Needless to say, he figured out what I did with his visiting hours. The fact that he appreciated my insight into his problem and my taking the time to help was all the reward I needed. The "crisis" turned out to be a strengthening factor in our relationship.

Whatever the crisis, you must—if you take your marriage vows seriously—stand by him and help him get over his feeling of hopelessness. Help him see that he *will* recover. Help eliminate his fears. Pray with him for guidance.

When you handle a crisis well, you show your husband that he can trust in your love for him, that it is your love, and God's grace, that carries him through. You reassure him by nourishing his good opinion of himself. At the same time, you add another strenthening bond to your relationship.

## *Are You Unintentionally Cruel to Your Husband?*

A woman in love can be cruel to her husband and not even know it. Of course, if she snaps, puts down, teases offensively, or threatens, she certainly is aware of it. These are self-indulgent outlets for her own frustrations and irritations. They have nothing to do with her husband's behavior.

If you want to secure a healthy and happy relationship with your husband, make sure you check out your behavior. The one you love is always the easiest to hurt. It's because you love your man so much that you know all his vulnerable areas. Strangely enough, it's because you feel secure that you take the freedom to attack those areas.

If you are unhappy with something your husband has done, you should take it to him *privately*. Airing the problem in public means that you are subconsciously seeking sympathy and even support from others. But what usually happens is exactly the reverse. The sympathy goes to your husband because you have made him look foolish.

I have learned to think before I speak or act. I imagine myself in my husband's place and try not to make a remark I wouldn't want made about myself. Truly, it is as Jesus said: "Do unto others as you would have others do unto you."

The cruelty you inflict unintentionally is more subtle. For instance: Your husband takes you out for dinner. The two of you are sitting at the table talking, but you are surveying the people in the room instead of attending to what he is saying. This tells him that you are not as interested in him or what he's saying as you are in all the strange people in the restaurant.

He might feel you are looking for a new face to excite you. He may not say anything about it, but he certainly cannot feel that you "only have eyes for him" or that he is the most important person in your life.

You should look at your husband when he talks to you, even at home. Wouldn't you give a guest in your home that courtesy? Put your book or paper down when your man talks to you; give him your undivided attention. After all, if you don't give him your attention, he won't give you his.

Another form of cruelty is to talk about your old boy friends to your husband. Sometimes it's done only as another way of saying to your husband, "I must not be too bad since Tom liked me very much and he was very good-looking." But instead of building your image up, it makes you seem a little cruel. You are only hurting your husband. Every man likes to feel that he is the only one you really love—the only man in the world for you, his wife.

# 4

# The Playground of Marriage

## It's Okay

SO FEW WOMEN know today just what they are supposed to do in love-making. In the past they were told, Do nothing. He'll do it all. Women weren't supposed to enjoy sex. It was that "terrible price" a woman paid for a home and a family. If, heaven forbid, she actually liked anything beyond a chaste kiss, if she enjoyed getting into bed with her husband, something was wrong with her. But now we know that was all wrong. Pioneer studies in sexual relations have shown that women can and should enjoy sex, that there is nothing wrong with them if they do. And that if a woman has a problem with sex, a frank discussion with her husband, plus excellent counseling by a doctor or therapist, can overcome the difficulty and enhance that important part of her life.

Men need sex: so do women. Sex is vital to a marriage—for the wife as well as the husband. It is as wholesome an activity for her as it is for him.

The Bible states that the husband must give his wife what she has the right to expect, and that she must give the same to him; the wife has no rights over her own body, the husband has them; the husband has no rights over his body, the wife has them. In other words, sex is mutual. Sex is a man and a woman joining together, consummating their God-given love.

According to God's word, a woman's body was made for a husband's enjoyment, and a husband's for a wife's. How conveniently God arranged for our pleasure! He has made it clear that sex is a privilege and a delight.

"Find joy with your wife you married in your youth," it says in Proverbs. "Let hers be the company you keep, hers the breasts that ever fill you with delight, hers the love that ever holds you captive."

A world without sex would be a world without a future. That was *not* God's plan. He made the female attractive to the male to make sure that the species would propagate. And He made the act of propagation pleasurable. Would God have made sex so joyous, so pleasure-filled, if it were wrong? If he didn't mean for man and woman to enjoy it? No!

## It's Good for You

Having a good, mutually enjoyable sexual relationship with your husband is not only good for him; it is good for you. Love-making makes you feel more self-assured. It makes you feel more like a complete woman.

Sex is good for you. It's a part of you as much as your mind, body, and soul. Without sex you wouldn't be here.

I know when I'm having a well-balanced sex life, because I feel much better; and women I interviewed felt the same. It's a vicious (but sweet) circle. Sexual satisfaction makes me feel better about myself. I feel better about myself because my husband makes me feel desirable. When I feel desirable, I feel radiant, needed, attractive—I blossom. With sexual attention, the bud becomes a rose. How many times have you seen a timid young girl blossom after a short period of marriage? She becomes more sure of herself; her personality becomes more alive. She has learned about her desirability and she begins to look and feel better about herself.

Full beauty can be achieved only when the feeling of sexual frustration is lifted with a guiltless conscience.

The next day, the memory of the night before can give you much pleasure, which, in turn, makes your relationships with the people around you more satisfactory. Because your body is more relaxed, your day will be brighter and more successful.

## Your Role in Love-Making

When most women marry they are young, naïve, and innocent. Whatever they know about sex they have, unfortunately, picked up from whispered conversations with the girls. Mothers seldom speak openly about love-making, and if they do it is usually in negative terms. So the young woman entering marriage is shy and often ignorant, not knowing what to expect. The husband is often no better. His knowledge of love-making is usually sketchy.

But, during the early days, the couple comes to know each other physically as well as spiritually and emotionally. They learn about each other's bodies, learn to give and take pleasure, and eventually achieve a joyous union. Then, familiarity sets in.

Children come along. The husband's job becomes more pressured. Outside interests take up more and more of a couple's time. A husband returns home tired after a hard day, and is greeted by his equally tired wife. They pay less and less attention to one another. Love-making becomes ordinary, dull, boring. The couple loses sight of their own desires and pleasures.

Something must be done. And it is up to the wife, you, to do it. Bettering sexual relations is a wife's problem. She is the guardian of love . . . and part of love is sex. Now, it is hard to be the initiator; often it is difficult even to admit that there is anything wrong. But it is the wife's job.

The female body is sufficient to arouse a man's desire, but he needs more than that. If you just allow your husband to "take" your body, like a piece of furniture, the sexual union will not be satisfying for him. Your husband needs your active participation and your *enthusiasm*.

How often have you cooked a meal without being enthusiastic? What did it taste like? Dull and bland. Haven't you played a game of tennis or a hand of bridge without enthusiasm and lost? Don't lose your rightful moments of exquisite sex. Be enthusiastic. Approach sex with enthusiasm and your husband will respond accordingly.

In order to turn around a deteriorating sexual relationship, or to create a whole new satisfying one, a woman should be aware of two approaches. The romantic and the seductive.

First, the romantic. Most men aren't the hearts-and-flowers type. But that doesn't mean that you can't provide the little touches that can soothe your husband and provide an atmosphere conducive to love-making.

You can start romancing him when he's leaving for work. You know that he does not have time then, but you are giving him a promise of seduction for the very near future, if not as soon as he returns from work, then at bedtime. The fact that you initiate the seduction gives him considerably more excitement and pleasure—now he knows that you not only love him; you also desire him.

One night a week, try this. Feed the children early, before your husband comes home. Then take a long bath. Pamper your body by using a touch of bath oil or perfume in the water. Turn your thoughts to your husband. Think of your courtship; remember your early years of marriage. Try to recall him as a young man and yourself as a young woman. Say to yourself, "I am the lovely woman he fell in love with and married." If you had a pet name for him, repeat it to yourself. Relive your first kiss and embrace.

Now dress as if this is the most important night of your life. You want your sexiest outfit. Use perfume and do your hair in a soft and feminine style.

To your husband's favorite meal, that you've already made, add a bottle of wine. The table should be set with your best linen, china, and crystal. Put a bowl of flowers or a long-stemmed rose in a vase in the center. Candlelight is a must.

When your husband arrives, be waiting for him at the door. Have romantic music playing on the stereo or radio. Say to him, "I've waited all day for you to come home to me." This will be the start of a special, romantic evening.

The seductive approach is based on making your husband think you are craving him physically, so that he will then crave you. As we all know, after several years a husband can stop craving and start yawning. And why not? He's been used to seeing some witch climb into bed with him—an unsexy female with her hair in curlers and wearing the same ratty nightgown she's worn for months. When he leaves the house in the morning, Grumpy Gertie has her head in a cup of coffee. When he returns at night, he finds her in either an old housedress or old pair of slacks, slapping around the kitchen, in the mood for nothing more than a casual peck on the cheek—if that.

Okay, you say, but what about my husband? He goes to bed in the same underwear he's worn all day. He doesn't shower at night, and his beard is so heavy by ten o'clock that if I kiss him my face gets cut to ribbons. He doesn't get up in the morning saying he loves me . . . as a matter of fact, he doesn't say anything at all before his second cup of coffee, and then it's a complaint.

Well, I've heard about husbands like that. But would they be like that if their women were seductive, sexy, enticing? No way. If you want to change your husband into a loving dynamo, then step one is to change yourself.

In order to seduce him, you must know what turns him on. What pleases one man may turn another off. One man can be seduced by his wife's undressing very slowly, while another husband can be seduced by seeing his wife dress slowly—so that he can *then* undress her. Find out whatever intensifies your husband's pleasure and seduce him. *You* will love it.

Another of your roles in love-making is to let your husband know you love and appreciate his body. Let him know it gives you sexual pleasure. You can let him know this through words and by touching his body. Even if your husband doesn't look like a movie star, he still has something physically attractive about him. Maybe it's his eyes, or his mouth, or his legs. Whatever it is, tell him. And be sincere. No phony flattery!

Also, let him know he is a good lover, especially

73

when he pleases you the most. Respond to his love-making with joy. The more you respond, the more he knows you are pleased and the more pleased he becomes. Nothing is more satisfying to a man than knowing that his woman is enjoying the act of love with him.

Make sure you don't pretend an orgasm to bolster his ego. This only encourages your husband to have an orgasm before you are ready. Let him take the time you need for the most pleasure. And even if you don't have a climax, let him know that sex was very satisfying and exciting anyway.

Your role is to indulge in his sexual fantasies. The only stipulation is that you *both* must be able to enjoy the fantasy. If one of you has a fantasy that offends the other, then it would not be wise for the other partner to ask for that fantasy to be played out. But if he asks you to slowly take off black mesh stockings and a black bra with red trim in front of him or to make love *to him,* he is just a normal man. Play his love games with him, and tell him yours. Don't be shy about adult love games. Their rewards come in deeper mutual understanding and closeness.

Your role in love-making is to keep the communicative sexual lines open. You will share more physical enjoyment and love, because it will open a stimulating, fascinating playground of marriage.

## Your Sexual Capacity

Your husband has long been geared to playing the more active role in love-making, and he also finds it easier to obtain sexual satisfaction than you do.

Women have, until recently, played the more passive role, relying on their husbands to provide them with sexual satisfaction. Yet a woman's sexual equipment far surpasses the male's in body area . . . and a woman has higher sexual endurance.

Within the past ten years, the female orgasm has become a much studied subject. Before that, no one gave much thought to a woman's climax. If a woman did enjoy sex and had an orgasm, chances were that she was considered "loose," not quite nice.

Today the female orgasm is considered natural. It is the most desirable form of sexual satisfaction for a woman, a climax is to be sought not avoided.

Because of such studies as the one conducted by Masters and Johnson, many psychological barriers have disappeared, barriers that prevented many women from experiencing orgasm and truly enjoying sex. Masters and Johnson have shown how couples can help each other achieve orgasm. They have removed the mystery surrounding the female climax by making their studies on the subject available to the public.

It is now known that a woman is quite capable of moving from one orgasm right into another, while the average man is capable of one orgasm every fifteen or twenty minutes. If he is over forty, a man tires rapidly; a woman's age does not interfere with her sexual enjoyment.

Dr. David Reuben (in *Any Woman Can*) says, "Women can begin sexual intercourse sooner, do it more often, continue it longer and probably enjoy it more. The female capacity for orgasm is so great that it has never been fully measured. . . . Most researchers who have studied female sexual reactions allow their female subjects to reach about fifty consecutive orgasms and then discontinue the project in amazement. If a man can ejaculate five time in one colossal night, he is considered sensational—the woman he looks down on can reach five climaxes in a minute, take a sip of water, and go on to forty-five more."

Not only is a woman capable of sexual satisfaction, but the lack of it has been directly linked to irritability, insomnia, emotional upsets, headaches, and backaches. Freud has shown the harmful effects of sexual guilt and repression. Without sex tension mounts, and no psychotherapy or aspirin will bring relief.

However, you should not worry if you do not reach an orgasm every time you have intercourse. It is normal and even satisfying to miss on occasion. You are, after all, still basking in warmth, tenderness, and unity with your husband, and that is of primary importance.

Don't pretend to have an orgasm. A close relationship has no room for deceit. Always tell your man that you were fulfilled by his love-making. If he asks you if you climaxed, be honest—but add, "It still was a joy and a delight . . . I am content."

Never blame yourself or, worse, your husband for your failure to have an orgasm. If you rarely climax, talk to him about it. Perhaps you can try a new technique next time.

Whatever your reason for not climaxing, always consider yourself an equal partner in sex. Learn new ways to enjoy yourself with your husband.

## Communication Through Sex

You should think of sex as not only a physical necessity, but also, on a higher level, an important way to communicate with your husband. Sex is the primary and most elevated way in which you and your husband can communicate.

Intercourse is not simply a mechanical routine to relieve tension; it is an intense and personal connection. It is how a husband and wife can truly know one another. God's plan of perfection is the union of the two into one.

How can you communicate sexually if so far you've never gotten past a sexual whisper? Learn what pleases your husband and devote yourself to pleasing him. Wanting is the first step, but it goes with caring. You have to care deeply for your man, and a fulfilled, happy marriage must be the crown of joy you strive for.

During intercourse, become a part of your husband as he becomes a part of you. Express tenderness and warmth. Don't take sex for granted, and don't become a sexual robot, acting out all the steps of intercourse as if you and your man were playing a game of Monopoly.

Communication in sex is an exchange of feelings. And feelings should be acted out through touch. Let your fingers run gently over his body. Caress him. This tells him that you feel he is worth your total commitment. You care enough for his pleasure that you will take the time and effort to arouse his entire body.

And, if you allow him to tenderly explore your body, you are communicating trust to him. Relax. Don't be a frozen popsicle. Your husband wants to make love with a living, breathing, sensual *you*.

Freedom in touching, caressing, exploring, and sharing one another's body is the best way I know for husband and wife to communicate their love.

When you make love with your husband in a total, loving way, you are communicating that you accept him—as a man. It isn't easy to give up your inhibitions. Old habits die hard. But closeness means closeness of mind and body. Just remember that the Bible says a man and a wife must not refuse one another —except by mutual consent and then only for an agreed-upon time. Giving and taking. Only God could have arranged such a beautifully complicated physical and emotional union.

## Feminine Power!

Sex is one of the most important functions to your husband. You will do well to always remember this. Just because he doesn't tell you doesn't mean it isn't so. Don't make him suppress his feelings and desires. *Talk to him about sex.* It will free you from hesitations and inhibitions, and you will discover that it is easy to please him, to make him happy. And making him happy, in turn, makes you happy.

Being submissive to him gives you a kind of strange, warm power over him. Try seducing him for two weeks, until he is so exhausted *he* needs a rest for a few days. You won't believe the additional attention you will get. His mind will be on you when he's away at work. He can't wait to see what's next!

There is nothing wrong with "using" sex this way. Your husband loves it and God approves of it.

## Variety Is the Spice of Life

Variety in sex is his spice of life and can be yours, too, if you wish. And the rule is to *always* keep him guessing (but *only* in your sexual games with him. He should always be sure of you in every other way). Gradual loss of interest and boredom come with too much repetition of the same experience.

Why do you think many men are so fascinated by so many *different* women? It's because they are different. It's a change of pace. It's not knowing what to expect. It's a different point of view. It's something *new.*

I am *all* those women to my husband and it works.
I am Steve's "queen bee" (he told me so). I dare
you to use this theory, too. Change, change, change
—never be the same woman each week. One night,
I might wear a sexy negligee. On another, I might
do my hair in pigtails and have a pink bow tied
around my neck. On another, I might climb into bed
and ask him to undress me, or I might just start
undressing him. I've worn a plastic, see-through laundry bag with a ribbon around the waist to meet him
at the door.

Once, while Steve and I were sitting in a restaurant,
I was suddenly aware that I'd forgotten to put on
underpants. Embarrassed, I told Steve. He was so
delighted about it, I did it again and again. I told this
to a very close friend. She was with her husband one
evening in a restaurant when a woman came in wearing a very low-cut dress. Everyone was looking at
her, including my friend's husband. Remembering what
I had told her, she leaned over and told her husband,
"But I don't have underpants on." His eyes became
fixed on his wife. He completely forgot about the
woman in the low-cut dress. (She actually did have
underpants on, she told me, but went to the ladies room
and removed them so as to be able to live up to what
she had said!)

Finding new places in the house to make love is
fun. Think of one ahead of time; he'll love the
change. You can fill the tub for him (with cool or
luke-warm water—hot water weakens sexual urges)
and let him know you have drawn his bath. Then,
when he gets into it, wash him all over.

If you feel your own sex drives are not up to par,
there are several things you can do. First, make sure
you are not cramming too much into your day. Slow
down. Take a short nap before your husband comes

home. Stretch out with your feet up and close your eyes. Read romantic stories or novels (as Dr. Reuben suggests in *Any Woman Can*). Read part of a romantic novel each day.

The point is to *think more about sex*—with your husband. The more you think about it, the more you'll want and enjoy it. Think during the morning and afternoon how you would like your husband to make love to you that night and how you plan to make love to him. Tonight, you might ask him to start at your big toe and gently, with baby oil, massage your tense, overworked body all the way up to your neck. Then offer to do the same for him.

## Should You Be Your Husband's Mistress?

You are capable of possessing *all* the qualities a man looks for in a mistress, and you will have none of the disadvantages. I know that's a big statement to make, but read on and I'll show you how true it is.

First, what are the mistress's advantages? Why is she held in such high esteem in her man's eyes? Her sexual talents are only part of the relationship. Her other qualities are just as important to him. She has learned to listen to him, to build up his ego which perhaps has been trampled on by his wife. She is devoted to him, just as his wife is devoted to her children. She is patient and even-tempered. She cannot be possessive, jealous, or irritable. She cannot be tired when her lover is present. She works at making the time she has with her lover as perfect as possible. She gives herself completely, whereas he can only give part of himself (his wife gets the rest). The mistress must listen to all of his complaints about his work and his wife, his feelings of guilt about being with her. She sleeps with him, but gets up with him, too.

All those things *you* are capable of giving. Those qualities are in you—remember how it was when you first married him?

The mistress's disadvantages are absent for your life. Such as the fear that he will abruptly leave her. Being taken to only certain restaurants for fear of being seen. Not being able to call him at work. Not being able to have his children. Knowing she does not share his bed in a socially acceptable manner, that the relationship she has is an immoral one. A mistress is very often a deeply lonely person. She can never be jealous. If she doesn't keep her looks up or satisfy her man's needs, she will be instantly dumped.

All of the positive things a mistress has (and more) were what your husband found in you when he married you—and you still have them.

You have to keep the sizzle in your marriage. Keeping your husband happy at home and preventing him from straying is your obligation. And it's a full-time job. So put your energy into it. Make yourself desirable and delectable. Make your husband want to come home to *you* instead of staying out with another woman. If your man "plays around," it is your fault. You are the one he wants—you are the woman he married. So turn things around. Rekindle the light of love and desire in your husband's eyes.

Let me tell what one friend of mine did. She had a suspicion that her husband was being unfaithful. Rather than create a scene, pack up and leave, or even confront him with her fears, she took a long, hard look at herself. And she asked: Am I the same woman he married? Am I still desirable? Do I give him what he needs sexually? Her answers were all No!

So she decided to attack the problem at the most

vital point—sex. She knew that if her husband was straying, it was because he was bored with her sexually. And so, one day, she sent her children to visit their grandparents. That night when her husband came home, she was ready to be the new, exciting woman in his life.

She met him at the door in a skimpy, sexy gown that a lacy, demure little-girl robe hardly covered. What a contrast! She had her hair done just right, a gentle touch of make-up, and she was wearing a brand-new perfume. The moment he came through the door, she beckoned seductively with her finger.

Her husband was incredulous. But he followed her, as she kept looking back at him over her shoulder. In the bedroom there were fresh, sweet-smelling sheets on the bed. On the dresser were candles. A faint trace of incense was in the air. Except for the candlelight, the room was dark.

Slowly, she undressed her husband and drew him into bed. Well . . . I don't have to go on, you get the picture. Whether or not my friend's husband was straying, or even thinking about it, was now a dead issue. If he was, he isn't any more. Every week or so, my friend stages a scene for her man and, to hear her, it is, mutually, very rewarding.

## What Makes Sex Become Boring

There is no reason to have a boring sex life. But an exciting sex life is not something that just happens, at least not after the first few years of marriage. It must be worked at. This a normal approach for a normal problem.

We have grown up thinking that if it's "true love," we should automatically have an exciting sex life forever. We were never taught that any long-range relationship between husband and wife can lead to sexual boredom unless they work at maintaining the excitement. We were not taught to *expect* boredom, and therefore we are not prepared to work at preventing it. Before you can have an exciting sex life, you must know what causes a boring one.

We're like cats chasing our tails. We feel bored sexually, become tense and difficult to live with, which then causes an over-all breakdown in the marriage.

One of the main causes for a boring sex life is always knowing what to expect, developing a pattern that never varies. Sex becomes a routine. The same routine of *anything* year after year is boring. Why should sex be any different? If every Saturday night after the eleven o'clock news, you know it is time to make love, and you've made love on the same side of the bed in exactly the same way for the past five years—no wonder the excitement has faded! This does not make for deep marital happiness. Your husband becomes dissatisfied with his bedroom activity and you become depressed about his dissatisfaction. Nagging starts and it becomes difficult to reverse the whole chain reaction.

Sex can become exciting again—and you alone can have the ability to control this. Your husband will follow your new plan with amazing interest.

Again, the key word is change. Be flexible. Don't let an exciting sexual relationship pass you by. Make up your mind to plan a different love-making approach for several weeks. Buy new, sexy nightclothes, a seductive perfume, read a book on sexual relationships and talk it over with your husband. Make love in the morning or wake him up at night. Buy him red bikini underwear. Tell him you like his body.

But, above all, *talk to your husband*. Be frank

with him and ask him to be frank with you. Talk about your desires and fantasies. No matter how silly you think they are, try them once. Who knows, one of them may just be what you have been needing or wanting all along.

Many women are not being cruel in refusing their husbands sexual satisfaction—they are just not interested. And then they blame themselves. They think something is wrong with them, mentally or physically, when all it is is boredom!

## Body Signals

You will please and excite your husband by learning to express your desires through body signals. These signals are not exclusively for your most intimate times with your husband. Use them when it is not possible to make love at the moment. For instance, at the dining-room table, in a restaurant, while taking a walk, or in any public place.

Why give him body signals? To let him know you enjoy thinking of him in a sexual way. To remind him that you think of him for reasons other than because he brings home a paycheck. He will think much more of you for making him think so much of himself. And that's exactly what you are doing—making him feel better about himself. You are telling him that he is desirable as a male. Your husband loves to be loved and wanted for his sexual masculinity, as well as for his ability to provide.

I can catch Steve's eyes, that were only meant for a passing glance at me, and hold them on me by fixing my eyes on him. I can "refuse" to let his eyes leave me. With a slight smile from me, he knows what message I'm giving. That is, I'm looking at him as a *person* who has feelings, including sexual, and

I'm acknowledging them. I'm not looking at him as an object or as just a provider.

Another signal is letting your eyes roam his face, studying his lips or body. The situation will tell you how subtle you must be. But once you do this, he will be looking for other intimate messages. The more subtle these public caresses, the more exciting they are to him.

Your "innocent" hand in the neck of your blouse, or your fingers trailing nonchalantly across your breast, or a slight sway to your hips when you walk can give him your message. You are recognizing his masculine sexuality.

It's a game, a private game for both of you. Soon he will be giving you messages. It's a game you play to wake up each other's body. Of course, it may take a while for him to get the message if sex has been underground too long.

When your husband gives you body signals, respond in a way that shows him his attentions have affected your awareness of yourself. He will become more alive and attentive.

For subtle physical body signals in public, try "accidentally" brushing your body against his, touching the nape of his neck, or his arm, or touching his thigh with yours. Your more obvious body signals could be being temptingly dressed to greet him at the door, or wearing a sexy new perfume. His obvious body signals might be a bouquet of flowers, or helping you to finish up after dinner so you can relax or retire together.

## Your Bedroom

Your bedroom is the most important room in the house. In fact, the most important place in your life.

You spend about one third of your life in bed. You make love there, sleep and dream, and seek its refuge when you are ill.

The bedroom is more private and intimate than any other room. It's where you have some of the most pleasant and memorable experiences in your life.

Now, take a good long look at your bedroom. Go ahead, now. Take this book with you and check off mentally the answers to these questions.

Does it look like a place where the rest of the world can be forgotten?

Does it beckon you to rest?

Does it invite you to make love?

Do you have soft lights, music available, and smooth, clean sheets?

Is it a comfortable place to relax, with ample pillows?

Is it a private enough place where you both can indulge fantasies?

Does it look and smell like a romantic haven—are there flowers in the room?

Have you seen to it that you can read or watch TV without having to get up from bed to turn off the lights?

How is it to wake up in?

The room should be pleasant to wake up to. The shades should have been adjusted the night before so that you wake up comfortably and gently. The clock-radio should have soft music. The children should be trained not to enter your room unless there is an emergency, and then to knock first. Why not have a small refrigerator in your bedroom for juice, fruit, milk, or whatever you and your husband like to start the day with?

The bedroom is often the most neglected room in

the house just because it is private. Take a look at yours and see how it can be improved to give you and your husband the comfort you deserve. Make it a refuge—a place away from the cares of the world.

Take inventory of your husband's needs—what small items will give him more comfort? For example, Steve and I read a lot and watch TV in bed. I bought two extra pillows for more comfort. That gives us two large pillows each to lean on. Then I bought a baby pillow for the times when he has a backache. Since neither one of us likes to get up to turn the TV off, I bought a remote-control unit. I also put a faint scent of perfume on the sheets a couple times a week.

Make sure the sheets and blankets are large enough. That way, not only is your warmth during the night insured, but it might very well prevent a sheet or blanket argument.

The bedroom should be a place you and your husband look forward to sharing each night.

## The Sensuous Massage

The sensuous massage can be an erotic massage, creating a gradual anticipation of intercourse; it can also be used for nothing more than inducing total relaxation for you and your husband.

The sensuous massage, in addition to giving physical contentment to the body, also allows you to become more aware of your partner's body. The more you learn about each other's bodies, the more you can please each other while love-making.

If you have never experienced a sensuous massage, tell your husband you have a treat in store for him. Plan a time that is convenient for both of you. Start with a warm bath (together if you wish). Make sure the room is warm enough for complete nudity. The lighting should be soft, and music, if any, should be low so that total relaxation can be achieved. Plan ahead of time to talk during the massage.

Have baby oil and a towel ready by the bed. Use very little oil, just enough to smooth and soften the skin for easier massaging.

The art of the sensuous massage is always a gentle, slow, rhythmic movement. Ask your husband to first lie on his back and relax. Start with one foot. Rub gently and flex his toes. Then massage each toe separately. Rub his ankle bones with a circular movement —one hand on each side of the ankle. Move to the heel of the foot and then on to the sole. (If your husband comes home exceptionally tired, this foot massage along with a cup of tea or a glass of wine will rejuvenate him.) Next, bend one leg, knee up, and massage with long strokes, using both hands. When moving to the upper thigh, knead with your fingertips or knuckles. Do the other foot and leg.

Move to his arms next. Massage with gentle pressure and long strokes. Move to his hands and work on each finger separately, as you did his toes.

Massage his shoulders and chest with a firm hand. (When he massages your chest, he should use a lighter, more gentle stroke.) The stomach should be massaged gently, but firmly enough so you don't tickle. Tickling causes the muscles to tighten up.

Ask your husband to turn over. Massaging his back will relax him and also increase the blood supply to the main nerves in the upper part of his body. Use the weight of your body to press down on his. (But ask him not to press that hard on your back.) The lower part of his back is the more sensuous area. Massaging it can add more pleasure to the massage and will also relieve the backache caused by standing or sitting all day.

88

Next, massage his neck. Start above the hairline and work down to the bottom of his neck gently with your fingertips. The area on each side of the spinal column is a very effective massage area. Continue along the muscles of the neck to the top of the shoulders.

Massage his entire scalp with your fingertips. Don't miss the area right behind his ears and along the base of the skull.

Now it's your turn. Relax and enjoy it.

## Sex in the Afternoon—or Morning

The aphrodisiacs of lovers are *Imagination, Initiative,* and a *Sense of Adventure.* A lazy attitude toward love-making is definitely not conducive to a good marriage. Your husband is aware of this; he knows it takes hard work to do anything well.

Unorthodox times can make love-making more exciting. Love in the afternoon can be as exhilarating as a Christmas present in July. It's the unexpected that gives it that extra dash.

If you think of love-making as something that happens only at night, in bed, in the dark, then you are missing out on spontaneous, exciting, sexual fulfillment.

Now, I know there are problems—children around, housework routine, your husband works during the day. Those are logical reasons to postpone love-making until bedtime. But, with a minimum amount of planning, love-making can be done at an unorthodox time, which is *any other* time than the time you usually make love.

Getting away from your deeply entrenched habit of sex in bed at night will help you to get away from the feeling of often being too tired. If your day's work is not enough to tire you out, then the normal routine of your sexual relationship is. If you had to eat the same food for every dinner, no matter how much you liked it in the beginning, you would soon be bored, and eventually you might hate it.

The practical problem of afternoon love-making can be solved through planning. Either take the phone off the hook or don't answer it. Who's more important, the person on the other end of the phone or your husband? The doorbell can certainly be ignored. People should not just drop in, anyway. They should ask you first. People have no right to intrude whenever they please—so don't feel guilty about not answering. You only need to answer your husband and he's calling you at the moment.

If you have young children, you can perhaps arrange for a friend to care for them for an afternoon. If you have older children, just tell them you are taking a nap.

Making love in the afternoon can give you the sensation of partaking of a forbidden fruit. It's tantalizing. It's different. In Steve's business, it's often necessary to have long business lunches with clients —two hours is not unusual. Sometimes I invite him *home* for a two-hour lunch. I make sure the lunch is on the table and waiting when he arrives. That way I haven't wasted a minute of his time preparing lunch, which gives *me* time enough to seduce him. If it's absolutely impossible to make afternoon arrangements, then try setting your alarm a little earlier one morning.

Changing the pace, breaking the routine, is as important as changing positions and methods of love-making.

## *The Misunderstood Word: Frigid*

Marriage counselors, psychologists and experts like Masters and Johnson are taking the word "frigid" less seriously these days. The term, they say, is applied too freely.

There are not many women who are frigid in the true sense. More than likely, they are sexually withdrawn because of a problem they cannot solve or has not been solved for them. They are labeled frigid, because the end result the unsolved problem is that their sexual relationship with their husbands is not satisfying.

It's easy to pin the label frigid on yourself—but don't be so hasty. There are a multitude of problems that could be influencing you and most of them *can* be corrected. You might have the *symptoms* of being frigidity, but it is more than likely that the problem itself lies in another area.

If your sex drive is reduced or you have none at all, you should understand that there are logical reasons for it. If you can find those reasons, by talking to your doctor, marriage counselor, or husband, you will probably find you are *not* frigid after all. But you *must talk* to someone about it.

Let me give you an example. About a year ago, my friend Louise changed the birth-control pills she had been taking for ten years. Her doctor thought the brand should be changed as a precautionary measure. About two months later she began to lose her normal sexual desires. She was worried—it was such an unusual experience for her. She just seemed to have no interest in sex. What could change her feelings so fast? Her relationship with her husband was excellent.

Be A Woman!

Perhaps this is what happens to everyone eventually, she thought. Should she just accept it? She decided it was much too important an issue. She went to her doctor, and in just about five minutes he had pinned it down to the new brand of birth-control pills. He gave her a new prescription (still different from her original one), and it solved her problem, which was an imbalance of hormones caused by the pill. (Not all birth-control pills cause this, and not everyone reacts the same.) Had she not been determined to find out the cause of her problem, she might have been labeled frigid forever.

Other logical causes are:

*Physical.* If intercourse is, or *ever* was, painful, then it's normal for you to have a fear of pain during intercourse. The chain reaction starts. You fear the pain, so you tense up your muscles, and intercourse becomes more difficult and painful. It's important to remember what is normal here. The pain is *not* normal, but if you have or ever have had pain, then the *fear* of it *is* normal. The point is to discover the logical cause of the pain so you can relax and enjoy sex.

Talking with your doctor, explaining your fears, can help him give you the answer. Also talking to your husband, opening up to him, confiding in him, will make him want to be more patient and understanding and perhaps more gentle. But you *must* communicate and not keep the fear bottled up in you. Maybe you and your husband will find he is too rough or, because he is too eager, he's too fast and rushes you. Talking to him will enable you to relax and enjoy the pleasure.

Just remember that your reaction to pain is normal; there is nothing wrong with you sexually. Irritations or pelvic pain should never be ignored. See your doctor at once for treatment.

*Psychological.* The will to solve the psychological problem must again start with communication. This word "communication" is the key to the problem's solution. It isn't always easy, but if you can force yourself to open up, you are halfway home. If you don't begin to do something about your own problem, the result will be even more of a lessening of sexual response, until finally there is no sexual activity at all.

You use your body for sex, but it's really all in your head. Your brain is your most vital sexual organ—what you do depends on what you *think* about sex when you are having it, as well as when you are not. You can't reach a climax if you let your thoughts wander. Your body is in bed and your mind should be, too—not out in the kitchen.

*Fear of Pregnancy.* Before contraception became so available, the thought of becoming pregnant was a great psychological barrier to sexual enjoyment for many women. If you are not too sure of the methods you use, it can still cause a problem. Check with your doctor and make sure you are using the best method for yourself, one that you have confidence in.

*Exhaustion.* This is an obvious logical sex depressant. If it happens once in a while—as it will, to both you and your husband—don't worry; it happens to everybody. You have children, a home to care, dinner to prepare, and most probably some outside responsibility—a hobby, PTA commitments, church work—so it's logical for you to be tired by the end of the day. But if you *always* seem to be too exhausted, then find out why. Maybe you need to check your diet, your vitamin intake. It is possible you could need more iron and $B_{12}$. I take $B_{12}$ and iron, and it *does* make a difference in my energy level. Ask your doctor's advice.

*The Absence of Orgasm.* This is no reason to label yourself frigid, either. If you *talk to your husband,* ask him to try different techniques to help find out what you like most, you will eventually find what can give you a complete orgasm. The point here is that you may appear frigid, but with the right experimentation you will very likely find that you are not. (A cake will not rise without *all* the proper ingredients.)

Women, unlike men, can enjoy intercourse without reaching a climax all the time. And certainly, you don't have to reach an orgasm at exactly the same time your husband does. It's fine if it happens; but it should not be your goal, because it means that you would have to make a conscious effort in an act that should be spontaneous.

*Living with In-laws.* If living with your in-laws prevents you from relaxing while having sexual relations with your husband, plan to make love at times when they are not there and see how "unfrigid" you really are! When you know you are not frigid, you will be able to gradually overcome your tensions and make love even when they are in the house.

*Children.* Interruptions caused by the needs of children are a logical problem. It's not always an easy one to solve, but planning ahead does help. And remember, they will grow up soon enough.

You may not be able to change all of these matters immediately, but understanding them and talking them over with your husband will make you feel better about yourself. At least you will both know you are not frigid, that it's only a matter of time and/or change. Communication is the basic sexual technique to employ between you and your husband. If you find it difficult to start to communicate, ask to see a marriage counselor. They can be most understanding, and remember that there is *nothing* that is new to them. They have already heard your story several times. So, don't be afraid to open up.

## Sex—Menstruation—Menopause

Many women suffer from premenstrual tension. This can lead to depression, irritability, and lack of sexual interest or desire. But it does pass after a few days.

Letting your husband know when your heightened sexual desire occurs during your cycle will help him to pace his own desires. Your desire might heighten just before, during, and immediately after menstruation. Or you might be so uncomfortable just before or on the first day or two of menstruation that you can't stand to be touched. Your breasts might be extremely sore and your stomach and vagina tender.

Letting your husband in on your cycle changes will help him to know just how much more time you will need to be aroused. If you have stronger desires at certain parts of the month, it *is normal*. Letting him know will result in a greater pleasure for both of you.

For some women the middle and later years are the best times in their lives. Often for the first time, a woman truly discovers sex, and discovers also that she can and does enjoy it. I have a friend who is in her sixties. She and her husband struggled for a long time. They raised four children and had to deal with many personal tragedies. Twice his business suffered losses so severe that the future looked black indeed, but both times he managed to pull out. Suddenly, fortune seemed to shine on them. The business became successful and stayed that way. Their children grew up and went off to college. "For a moment," she told me, "I panicked. Here I was, finally without any great worries and very few responsibilities."

Their sexual relationship during the years of struggle was, according to my friend, very fragile. Perhaps it was because of all the tension, the continual trauma they went through separately and together. She had, though, come to accept this part of her life as not particularly satisfying. And then things began to change. She was freer, more relaxed. She could now devote time to understanding herself as a sexual being, to considering how her husband felt about sex. Steeling herself for a rebuff, she approached him to discuss sex. Surprisingly, he was very open. No, he hadn't been happy with their sexual relationship for a long time. But, like her, he had come to accept it. After all, they had survived so much, and the rest of what they shared was deeply satisfying.

From this initial conversation, they went on to further discussion. They began reading books together, such as Dr. David Reuben's *Everything You Always Wanted to Know About Sex . . . But Were Afraid to Ask,* and talking over what they learned. From their reading and their talks, they gained a more relaxed intimacy. And, after a while, they began to enjoy each other as they never had before.

It wasn't until after menopause that my friend achieved her full sexual potential and began to please her husband as he deserved to be pleased. She is not the only woman I know for whom this is true.

So, you see, the old feeling that a woman loses sexual desire at menopause isn't true. It's really an old wives' tale. If a woman loses her desire at menopause, it is purely psychological. She is probably looking for an excuse. She may feel there is something "wrong" with older people making love. But love-making can become even more deep and beautiful at that time in your life.

It has been established that many women associate the loss of fertility with a loss of sexual desire and attractiveness. It is true that, for a short time, some women have fewer sexual desires but, with the help of their doctor, it is not necessary to go through the unpleasantness of this phase. Many times the lack of sexual desire is caused simply by tension and fear of menopause.

The woman who keeps herself desirable and realizes that her husband does not associate her fertility with his desire for her will pass through this stage in her life unmarred.

The menopause is not the "end," it's the "beginning." Think positively about it. Not having to worry about a monthly cycle, the freedom from the fear of getting pregnant, and the relief of not having to use contraceptives can heighten a woman's sexual response.

Many doctors are giving women the female hormone estrogen at this time of their lives. It helps to eliminate the side effects of menopause and also helps them to maintain a better relationship with their husband during this time. Check with your doctor—it may be the best thing you can do for your marriage at this time.

Menopause is really a time that should be looked upon as the beginning of a new phase in your life. It is the beginning of a new freedom that can be turned into the best years of your life through more companionship, love, understanding, and sexual harmony.

## *Your Husband's Impotence—It's Your Problem, Too*

Your husband's failure to achieve an erection can threaten his entire sense of identity, causing both physical and psychological problems for him and a feeling of rejection for you.

Most men, at one time or another, have experienced impotence. But when it happens to your husband, it seems to be impossible for him to look at it objectively. He becomes too concerned with the moment, which causes even more anxiety.

It is most important that you do not unintentionally show overanxiety for him. If his problem is not deeply seated, and most likely it is not, then a willingness to learn and understand his emotional attitude and physical responses will go a long way toward giving his male identity back to him. Also, paying more attention to your appearance, your attitudes toward him in general, and to your sexual techniques with him may help.

This is a very difficult situation for any woman to be in. First of all, you can become angry: your husband has let you down. But don't be. No man wants this to happen to him and he is always horrified, confused, and upset. Your getting angry just makes the situation worse. He now has to handle his sexual problem, but also the problem of your anger. And on top of that, he undoubtedly feels guilty.

You mustn't nag him, either. Don't criticize, downgrade him, or question his masculinity in any way. Try to put yourself in his place. How would you feel if suddenly you lost your potency? Pretty awful.

Some impotence is short-lived and can be traced to things like drinking too much, a sudden change or crisis at work or in the family, being overtired, too many pressures all at once. Being understanding at these times can only make for a deeper long-range relationship. Give him support and put your own needs and desires aside. It will pay off tremendously in your future relationship.

If the problem of impotency persists for a long period, the help of a doctor should be sought. He will help your husband get to the root of the problem. That, plus a complete love and trust from you, will get your husband back to his full sexual potential.

According to studies, a loving honesty in discussing the problem and re-establishing a pattern of physical loving are more necessary than the actual sex act.

Therapists strongly recommend that you use no genital play in the beginning of building your husband's confidence back up. Only embracing, back stroking, and tenderness in general are advised. Even if your husband wants to make love at this point, it is recommended that you both refrain from full intercourse.

When you both finally decide you are ready for full intercourse, then let your husband take your hand and show you what is most pleasing to him. Remember, your goal for the moment is to help him gain confidence. Your needs for sexual fulfillment should take second place until after you both have reestablished a pattern of sexual competence.

Your husband may need you to fulfill his sexual fantasies to help get him going again. If lace-and-satin undergarments excite him more, for heaven's sake, go out and buy them. He will love you forever for giving him back his old self-image.

With a great deal of patience, generosity and self-control, *you* have the power to return to him his most important possession—his maleness.

# 5

# Occupation: Homemaker

## The Two Most Important Jobs in the World

MY FRIEND NANCY was married to Herb for three
years—and what a stormy three years they were!
Herb is a self-made man, a dynamo who built a small
plumbing-supply business into a good-size corpora-
tion. By working long hours and devoting himself to
his business, he gained a successful career, but he
didn't have the time for a wife and family. So it
wasn't until Herb was in his thirties that he married.
He and Nancy had a whirlwind courtship. Whenever
I saw Nancy in those days she was beaming—and
why not? She had a handsome, affectionate man who
treated her with love and respect. Then they got
married.

The first few months were idyllic because Herb
continued to treat Nancy like a princess. Whatever she
wanted was fine. And Nancy, becoming more and
more self-occupied, forgot that Herb was her husband, with a demanding career, worries, stresses, and
strains.

Herb would come home from the office and Nancy
would be lying on the couch reading a book. Dinner

was never ready; the house hadn't been properly tended to. Why should she exert herself? Wasn't she a princess with a man who adored her no matter what?

Well, no matter how much your man adores you, he is the breadwinner, the head of the house, the one who must face the grueling outside world—and he wants a haven, a refuge in his own house.

Herb didn't want to go out to dinner every night. He didn't want to find the breakfast dishes still in the sink, because Nancy had spent the day shopping with the girls. A storm began to brew. Nancy fretted. She couldn't understand, she'd tell me, what happened to Herb.

No matter how much I explained to Nancy that though Herb needed to give her his loving care, and wanted to, she was not a pet or a princess. She was a wife and had a role to fulfill. She and Herb had a marriage contract and she wasn't filling her part of the bargain. "But," she'd insist, "I haven't changed. I'm still the woman he married." She was the same woman all right, but she wasn't a wife.

And so the marriage broke up.

A sad story, but true, and one that is repeated over and over again by women who don't understand what it means to be wives. Being a wife is the most important job in the world and a woman should take it seriously.

Most women do take motherhood seriously. In some cultures, women bear children and then leave them at day-care centers or nurseries or relatives while they work in the fields. But we're lucky in our society, because we are able to remain with our children, watch them grow, enjoy their stages of development, and have the opportunity to teach and guide them in the way we see fit.

Stop for a minute and think how important your mothering really is. You hold in your hands a being that is dependent on you for emotional growth, intellectual growth, physical health, and survival. This responsibility is solely yours until your child reaches school age, and then you share that responsibility with the teachers.

School increases the child's intellectual growth; the outside associations with people will have a big influence on his emotional growth. But you have set the foundation and your nurturing is still very necessary until your child goes into the world on his own. By that time, you hope you have produced a worthwhile human being who will be an asset to society. Years of your tender care have shaped his attitudes, beliefs, and goals. Can you see why we mothers are mainly responsible for the outcome of the next generation and their society?

Granted, fathers and outside influences have an enormous effect on that outcome; but, if we have taken our role seriously from the birth of the child and have managed to maintain a close, loving relationship with him, it is our influence that will be strong enough to keep him on a positive, constructive path.

Your role as homemaker, as wife and mother, might now begin to sound bigger and more impressive to you. Maybe you have been thinking of it as being too mundane and routine, but let me tell you something. I can't think of any job on this earth, including movie star, model, or company executive, that does not sooner or later get down to mundane details and routine. There are few people who don't have to deal with them. Details and routine—they are part of the fabric of life. But they are part of a whole that is satisfying to you, the woman, and necessary to all of society.

God didn't create man to be alone. He meant him to have a wife. And children are dependent and needy; they cannot survive without mothering. Only a woman can fulfill both these sacred functions and she should be proud of that.

## Homemaker-Executive

Homemaking is as skilled and valuable an occupation as that of a secretary, teacher, and company executive all rolled into one. Did you know it would cost well over $10,000 a year to have someone else come in to take over your responsibilities? Marylin Bender, in a *McCall's* article entitled *Money Talks*, came up with these figures for 1974. (Needless to say, they are even higher today.)

| Position | Rate per hour |
|----------|---------------|
| Nursemaid | $2.00 |
| Cook | $3.25 |
| Laundress | $2.50 |
| Gardener | $3.00 |
| Chauffeur | $3.25 |

Her findings brought the housewife's economic value up to $257.53 a week or $13,391.56 a year. This figure does not seem to include a general-cleaning rate, which would substantially increase the figure. I present these figures not so that you will have something to flaunt to your husband, but, rather, to prove to you that your occupational value is quite high. Don't underrate yourself!

The jobs mentioned are only the ones that would have to be handled by someone else if you had to work full time outside the home. In addition to those is the impressive gamut of other positions the average homemaker fills, such as: seamstress, secretary (to the husband), social director (for the family), shopper, nurse, teacher (of the children), and administrator (of the home.) Now, does this give you a higher image of your profession as homemaker? It should! What other occupation or profession requires the varied skills of the homemaker? No one could afford to pay for her value. It is a profession to be proud of and one that your husband can be proud of you for, if you handle it like a professional.

You might also keep in mind that your profession is somewhat easier today than it was for your sisters of a hundred years ago. They were expected to spend one third of their lives producing children. Today we spend one fifth of our lives procreating. Contraception has given us more control over the number of children we bear.

We also have the help of all kinds of machines our predecessors didn't have. The washing machine and dryer, toaster, mixers, dish washers, vacuum cleaners, the automobile, et cetera. With all of this help, your occupation has been modernized, giving you more time for self-expression through hobbies, further education, recreation, and whatever else you find is necessary to keeping your total identity intact.

One other point to remember is that we women are judged on our own merits today. Years ago, a woman was judged by the status or position of her husband —if she was married to a baker, she was "the baker's wife." If she was married to a doctor, she was "the doctor's wife." Today, women can stand on their own and be judged as individuals. We can be respected for the creation of a comfortable and relaxing home for our husband and children.

## *Homemaker versus Housewife*

Our housewife duties may have been downgraded—but don't you think we have done most of it ourselves? We feel inadequate because there is no degree attributed to homemaking. Let me remind you that God gives us our degree. We were born with instinctive qualifications and have spent our entire lives developing them. And our husbands appreciate our abilities, whether they say so or not. It is natural for women to be homemakers, and you should be proud in knowing that your profession is the *most important* of all.

As it says in Ecclesiasticus, "Like the sun rising over the mountains of the Lord is the beauty of a good wife in a well-kept house."

I would like to take the word "housewife" out of your vocabulary. I certainly don't use it. I learned that it has a negative image. Yet, if I say to someone, "I'm a homemaker," with a smile on my face, he or she knows that I'm proud of my job. People get the message—that I enjoy taking care of my husband and family (and automatically my husband and I gain more respect).

If your husband ever says of you "She's just a housewife," maybe it's because you have undermined your own job. Thinking back to the earlier years of my life, I can remember answering "Only a housewife" when I was asked what my occupation was. I gave my answer almost apologetically and thereby revealed my low esteem of the job. My point is, maybe we are responsible for downgrading our public image. If you start believing that being a *homemaker* (not a housewife) is a rewarding occupation, your public image will change.

I remember when, at a party, a business associate of my husband asked him what my occupation was. I piped up before Steve could answer and said proudly, "I'm a homemaker!" Jokingly, I was asked if that was the same as a housewife. I explained, in a serious tone, that it was basically the same, but that I approached homemaking as a business, an occupation, just as a man did his business. Well, the next thing I knew, Steve's friend had brought his wife over from the other side of the room and was asking me to give her some "business hints."

We can learn a lot from our husbands by developing a professional attitude and approach to our occupation. I have learned from Steve to be highly organized and to put things in their order of importance. He was pleased, because order is something he relates to. By taking my job as a homemaker seriously, as the respectable profession it is, I have gained my husband's admiration, and he acknowledges my accomplishments with love and affection. Now that I talk in his language and I find him more willing to discuss "business."

## The Organized Homemaker

If you take a professional attitude, your workday will be much more productive. You'll be less tense, have fewer disasters throughout the day, and finish on time. Then, with a clear mind, a smiling you can meet your man at the door when he comes home.

What is a professional attitude? For one thing, it's being goal-oriented. To start at the beginning and *finish* at the end. To stick to job until it's done. A professional attitude is, Do it now—get it done. Men see the end *first*, know exactly what *really* has to be done, and *stay with it*. You'll find that once you stay with the professional approach, you will have more time for fun activities, including your husband. You'll accomplish much more, and a new approach will surely get your husband's approval.

Just to check it out, I asked Steve for a man's definition of a professional approach. He said, "Professionalism is an attitude. It's attaching prime importance to the job and not letting fluctuations in mood dictate your performance. You must accept the fact that your activities are always part of a much larger machine. If you fail in your task, you are dragging down others with you. You must isolate the work responsibility from the rest of your personal life. Working is a continual learning process, there is no end to it. The result of this is commonly known as experience and it is what separates the men from the boys. Those who succeed in business are essentially *problem solvers*. People often confuse *defining* a problem with *solving* a problem. It is one thing to be able to discover a flaw or problem, but it is something else entirely to have the marvelous capacity to solve it."

I was almost sorry I asked him! Anyway, that is Steve's opinion of a professional approach or attitude. I do think it's a good one, don't you? He taught this attitude to me many years ago, and I can tell you it *does* work!

All professional men keep a calendar—hour by hour. Without my calendar, I would be lost. My calendar "remembers" for me. It helps me stick to my schedule and remembers what comes first and next. As I finish each item listed, I cross it off. It's a great feeling to cross off something that had to be done. You start to see your progress, which gives you incentive to continue.

Some days will be busier than others. If a friend

calls me up for lunch, I refer to my calendar. It might mean having to tell her that "today is too tight, but next Tuesday is open and would be great." Just because I am home does not mean I am automatically available every time someone calls and can forget my professional duties.

If you start using a calendar, it will soon get out that you follow a schedule. Your friends will start asking when you will be open for lunch or some other social activity. It's more fun to have lunch with a friend when you know the time has been set aside for it and you're not taking yourself from something that has to be done.

Organize to suit your own personal needs. I like to cram for several days so that I can have an extra day off. But I can handle it. One reason is that I've been using an organized calendar for many years. Another reason is that I have learned to take efficient short cuts. My two sisters are the same way. My mother, on the other hand, prefers to have a little more time off each day. She would rather not rush so much. It's a very personal thing. We all have certain tasks to perform and are fortunate that we can arrange our days to suit us. Our men work with other people and many times do not have the option of arranging their time to suit themselves.

One point to remember is never to set impossible targets or goals for yourself. That can give you as much nervous tension as having no direction at all. It can also hurt your relationship with your husband and children. Be realistic in your daily schedule. Be flexible. Anticipate the possibility of your schedule's being interrupted. If you have numbered your activities for the day in order of importance, the interruption should not throw you too much—and you will have mastered the art of organization.

Now I know most women have an average of two hours' work after five. But, if this "no pay" moonlighting is handled right, there'll be no reason to feel overworked.

Between dinner, the dishes, and a few extra chores, it's about seven before you can call it a day. Moonlighting with no pay? Not really, because you have the advantage of being able to "split shift," plan each day to replace those two hours of work *after* five with two hours of whatever you want *before* five.

If you follow my organized plan closely, it will be possible to have that time on most days. On your calendar take two hours off for whatever you would like to do. Your hobby, a nap, writing personal letters, exercise program, making clothes, reading, talking to a girl friend, whatever pleases you. It's *your* time.

Doing the split shift won't make you feel overworked at five. You can always fit in your hair appointment or your visit to the dentist, during your workday, while your husband usually has to do an extra activity *after* five. So, if you look at it honestly, it's not a bad deal. There are many, many things you can do during the day that he cannot.

There is nothing wrong in keeping your home in top condition. Your man will love it, too—providing your work doesn't replace time spent with him and he can feel comfortable living in his home. A home should always be clean and neat, but there must also be a relaxed atmosphere.

If you find you are continually fussing around the house when he's home—cleaning, dusting, emptying ashtrays after every cigarette, putting away magazines and newspapers as soon as someone has put them down—you are putting housework ahead of your husband. The house is a place to *live*. Don't make him feel as though he's living in a suite of department-store model rooms, where nothing is ever out of place. Let your man feel relaxed in his home so he will love to come home to you.

If you are well organized, you will know exactly what you must do throughout your day so that, when your husband comes home, you can relax *with* him after dinner. You will feel less resentful and the togetherness while relaxing will prove very rewarding.

It's not really that difficult to become well organized. It's quite possible that you are less organized than you should be, rather than genuinely overworked. If you find your day too short for the work you must do, these "organizers" will help you to complete your day with time to relax:

*The Calendar.* As I mentioned before, my calendar is the most important tool of my organization. For years, I've kept a calendar that shows one entire month at a time. I know by glancing at it what I must do for the entire month—even if it's just returning a phone call on a certain date. It's the most comforting feeling to rely on this calendar. It's my household "security blanket." I never have to clog my mind with "items to remember." (Your husband's boss never has to remind him—he's *expected* to remember.) When I think of something I should do, or want to do, I jot it down on the memory calendar. From "clean out my husband's closet, wash my hair, do the laundry" to "have lunch with Vernice"—it's all there. The night before, I number this list in order of importance. Then, if I cannot complete everything, at least the most important things get done.

As each item is completed, it's crossed off. What a feeling of success to see everything crossed off at the end of the day! But you must do this *every* day, even weekends. You can draw a line all the way down your weekend days that says "days off." Unless you have a dinner at Aunt Ruth's and Uncle Frank's, then write it in and put the time you are expected to be there.

*Children as "Helpers."* Young children love to help with anything and, as they get older, they can be trained to be of real assistance. If they get an allowance, then teach them to "produce" or "no pay." They will have to learn it soon or later; the earlier, the better.

Give them either a daily or a weekly list. Also ask them to be available for a half hour every day for small projects you might need done. Explain to young children that everybody must work together and help each other out. Daddy is out working for us and Mommy cooks and takes care of the needs at home for us. So would they please take out the garbage each day for us and make sure their toys are picked up by five for us. You can make them see that a family is like any working business. Everyone works together at what they can do best. That way, no one is overworked and things get done faster, leaving more time for fun.

*Cut Down Phone Chats.* If it's not an emergency, do what our husbands must do at work, say, "I'm sorry but I can't talk at the moment, can I call you back later or tomorrow?" If you are spending an hour on phone "chats" each day, that's almost one working day each week.

*Prevent Unnecessary Interruptions.* If someone drops over unexpectedly, you have every right to say that they caught you in the middle of doing "whatever" and could you call them at home and make an appointment when it is convenient for both of you. Chances are they will understand that they should always call you from now on and let you be included in their plans to visit you.

*No Trial and Error.* If you are short of time or don't know the right way to tackle a problem, ask someone who knows and do it properly the first time. Think things through!

*A Short Nap.* Five or fifteen minutes flat on your back will refresh you tremendously. You can then go back to work with a more relaxed body and attitude. I do this every day, sometimes twice a day. You want, above all, to be refreshed for your husband when he comes home.

*No Postponing.* Do it now! Postponing saps your energy, robs your peace of mind. But getting it done—crossing it off your calendar—gives you a feeling of accomplishment and the incentive to go on. The feeling is great!

## What Your Man Likes Most in the Home

The things that are important to you in the home are not necessarily important to your husband. That has more advantages than disadvantages. If you want to cut down on general housekeeping and keep your man happy at the same time, there are only a few things you have to remember.

Keep things "picked up" in general. He doesn't like clutter. Most men appreciate things being kept in their right place. A man is tired at the end of a busy day and he won't enjoy seeing a toy or the vacuum in the middle of the floor, furniture out of place, or your underclothes hanging in the bathroom. He also likes to come home to clean ashtrays, fresh-cut flowers sometimes, but *never* furniture rearranged. Your job is to make him comfortable, not dislocate him.

His chair should be empty *before* he walks in the

door. Children should be informed that the chair belongs to the "top brass" whenever he's home. They should be trained from early childhood that their father does not have to ask for *his* chair. No objects left in his chair for him to remove, no ice cream dripped on the cushions. I was taught at an early age that my father's favorite chair in the living room was "up for grabs" during the day, but when he came home, it was the "King's chair." We all knew it and respected him enough to make sure it was free of debris and ready for him to use upon his arrival.

His favorite objects should be kept in their place, where he can always find them when he wants them, preferably on a small table within reaching distance from his favorite chair. His pipe, cigarettes, matches, clean ashtray, TV guide, newspaper (folded like new), magazines—whatever he needs and wants should be easily accessible. And, most important, don't use your husband's belongings without asking him first. If he says okay, then be doubly sure that it is back in it's proper place by the time he looks for it.

If there is only one television set in the house, it belongs to the adults. Make sure the children understand that this is Dad's time to relax. He needs this time to prepare for the following day, to unwind from the pressures of the business world. He shouldn't have to argue with the children for his favorite show.

His bed should always be well made and, of course, with fresh linens. The bottom sheet should be well fitted to the mattress so it doesn't wrinkle up under his body when he sleeps. Also remember to make room for his feet at the bottom. Tucking in the bottom of the top sheet too tightly makes it uncomfortable for his feet, particularly if he is tall.

If you really want to spoil him, make sure he has *two* pillows. One to sleep on, two for comfort while reading or watching TV in bed. If he does not object to sleeping on a very small pillow, get him one. It will help his neck and back in the long run. (But don't force it on him.)

Privacy is most necessary for your husband. He may need fifteen minutes or two hours; but, after being talked at and to all day, he needs some time alone. He might need privacy upon returning home or later on during the evening. Ask him. My husband needs about twenty minutes to nap when he comes home from work and then ten minutes for his mail. Your children should be trained to allow him this time of rest and privacy. They shouldn't attack him when he comes through the door (and neither should you), except with smiles, warm hellos, and kisses. Your children will learn respect for other people's feelings this way.

If your man is the kind who prefers not to pick up after himself, then you do it. That's your job. Don't try to make him superneat if he's messy. Try to overlook it and think of his better qualities. If you leave a chair in the bedroom or a valet to throw things on, it might solve his problems and yours. After having been so disciplined all day, some men must let go at home. That's about the only place they can totally relax. If he feels he can't relax in his own home, you can be sure he will find a place elsewhere to do "his own thing." Maybe even find a woman who will willingly pick up after him or just ignore his untidiness. Remember, nagging won't change him; it will just make you look like a shrew.

All his belongings should have a place—his socks, shirts, razor, brush, clippers, et cetera. These are his "personal" belongings and should not be used by anyone else. Would you like someone using your toothbrush, comb, or facecloth? Well, he doesn't either. He

114

won't appreciate using a razor with a blade that is dull because you used it on your legs and underarms. You should have your own. Children should also be taught that someone's personal property means "hands off." Another lesson in respect for others.

If he has a workshop, den, or sitting room of his own, it should be cleaned, but his work projects should remain *untouched*. These areas are also "off limits" to the children unless Dad gives his permission otherwise. I don't let anyone touch Steve's desk. Even when I clean it, every paper, pencil, or whatever is left as I found it.

In general, if you want to know how he likes his home, go and visit his mother's home—that will tell you everything. The life style he grew up with and will probably feel most comfortable with, is the one you want to duplicate.

A drink when he comes home from work (milk, tea, coffee, Scotch . . .) will make him feel like he's Cary Grant. He feels about himself the way you feel about him. Bringing a drink to him tells him that you appreciate the hard work he has been doing all day for the benefit of his family. Steve doesn't want a drink the *moment* he comes home but after his nap and his mail, he loves the drink I give him before dinner. It tells him I'm thinking of him and that I care.

## Why Most Men Want Their Wives to Stay Home

Many men are opposed to their wife's taking a job outside the home. They insist that "a woman's place is in the home" or "the children will suffer."

But what are the *real* reasons? Reasons they won't

express to us or may not even be consciously aware of.

One is that it will make him feel inadequate as the breadwinner, that his wife is not satisfied with his ability to earn or with the way of life he has provided for her. *His* mother stayed at home while his father supported his family successfully. He is trying to live up to his father's image as the sole provider. Man is created in God's image, and God is the Creator and the Provider. That's the way it should be.

If his wife goes to work, a man loses some authority around the house; he even has to pitch in with the housework. She, as a working wife, threatens his position at home and as a male. His security about his own worth is at stake. He sees her as asking for her independence from him or maybe even as finding a new male to replace him.

Then there are the practical things. He won't be able to find clean socks or shorts, or he may be forced to have TV dinners instead of home-cooked meals. The house will not be kept as well and, of course, he worries that the children will suffer in many ways. He fears that she will no longer devote her time to caring for him or sharing his free time. A working wife can present a lot of problems to the whole family, as well as to herself. When I was working full time as a model, I did not have the time to cook and take care of my family in the way I wanted. My husband would often be out of socks or undershirts; I would find myself out of milk after the stores were closed. It's difficult to keep it all together when your interests are divided. And it is unfair to your husband and children.

Working outside the home is hard enough to cope with if your husband is encouraging you, but if he's not, the pressures at home can be more unbearable for you than those at the office.

At home you know what to do for your family. At the office, you will be told what to do for a vague, impersonal company. You go from the position of administrator of your *own* home to a subordinate position of working for someone else.

Then, what about the school holidays or when the children are ill—who will take care of them? You will be torn between your obligation to your job outside and the guilt feelings of not being home when needed. Your husband and children will sense your distress and suffer. If nothing else, you will become irritable and short-tempered as you try to be a split personality.

Yes, men are possessive and jealous, but is that bad? It does show they love us and don't want to lose us. And they want us to remain soft, feminine creatures.

## *If Your Husband Encourages You to Work Outside Your Home*

The two-career family is not an ideal situation. There are a number of problems to face. But if your husband is suffering a financial setback and *needs* or *wants* you to work and you are willing, then you must listen to him. He probably isn't happy about it, because a man's ego is bound up in being responsible for his family. So never throw this momentary dependence of his back in his face. Face the fact that you must help out and work together with him on solving the problems that arise.

Remember, even if he needs you and it's his suggestion, if you work, you are *still* challenging his position of authority as supporter and provider of the family. He will not be totally secure. Also, he and the children will not receive the attention and care they are accustomed to. Underneath it all, he still needs and deserves to feel that he is first. No marriage will work if a wife subordinates her husband to her job. The most honored titles a woman can have are wife and mother.

If you must work, remember the following: it is essential to set up a schedule for everyday routines. You cannot shirk your household chores. Be sure that you are superorganized so that you still have time to sit and talk to your husband, or just watch TV with him. Don't let your love life deteriorate because you have no time or are too tired.

Discuss any resentments or jealousies you feel your husband might have. When the feelings are in the open, they are easier to deal with and easier to solve. Ask him if he would like to take a weekend vacation alone with you. If you are working outside the house, you may be so busy with house and children when you get home that you fail to see your husband as that person you married. A vacation together can give you that time alone to "keep in touch." Most important—plan dinner for just the two of you whenever possible and meet for lunch. Treat him like a new lover. Put on that perfume you used to "catch him." Have shiny, fresh hair and wear a fresh outfit. Have occasional family dinners out or go on picnics. Order dinners in once in a while so you don't have to cook.

As for the children, spend time with each child alone, but don't *over*compensate by spoiling them. Make sure that they understand why you are working, and that the family is still your first priority. They shouldn't feel neglected. Talk to the children about your job. Help them to understand that their father's place has not been usurped and that he approves of your working.

Try to get reliable babysitters to help you fill the needs of your children. A young child needs a motherly woman. But the best babysitter in the world is still a substitute. You are the mother, and no one can or should take your place.

For a woman to work outside the home is not a desirable situation. A woman's obligations are to her husband and children. And a man's responsibility is to support his family. To tamper with an ideal situation is both dangerous and foolhardy. As a woman you will lose much more than you gain.

So even if the additional income may relieve financial pressures, quit if your job interferes with your prime functions as wife and mother.

# 6

# Making the Most of What You've Got

## The Beautiful You

WHEN YOUR HUSBAND first met you, he was physically attracted to you in some way. Maybe he was attracted to your rounded figure or maybe it's your classic nose he fell in love with. Whether it's a slim body, a very full figure, shining, healthy hair, or a small or large bosom, your husband married you because he liked *your* beauty.

Attractiveness does not depend on conventional good looks. Look carefully at many of the women on TV—study them. You will find that they are *not* all classic beauties, but they are attractive. They have taken what God gave them and they made the most of it.

The idea of beauty has varied for centuries, not only in different cultures, but also in different periods of history. Even within one culture the ideal of beauty has been known to change more than once.

In some cultures, beauty is an elongated ear and a gold tooth showing. In others beauty is dark hair with an elegant nose or a graceful mouth. Some people consider a long neck desirable, even using rings around it to increase its length. There are cultures that treasure dark circles under the eyes as a mark of beauty. Tattooing, blackening the teeth, carving designs on the skin, a flat chest, a very full chest, even fainting have at one time or another been considered necessary for beauty.

During the Renaissance, a woman was not considered beautiful unless she was very heavy. Look at the paintings of Rembrandt or Titian—the women are very large and soft, with rolls of fat.

So, if the idea of beauty varies so much from culture to culture, certainly your husband is entitled to his opinion. Think of what your husband loves about you most and play it up.

## Beauty We All Can Have

You can further improve yourself by checking out the following areas for improvement. Do *not* worry about your weak points. Pursue and play up your positive attributes instead.

*Your* voice is heard every day by your husband. What does it sound like to him? Women's voices (often unintentionally) are too high. Too shrill. If this is the case, do what my friend Ann did. She practiced speaking lower with me. She thought "lower voice" for several days until it became natural to do.

A lower voice is much more pleasant than a high one. It's easier to listen to and sexier.

If you have a montonous voice, practice to inject warmth and variety into it. Test your different voice levels on a tape recorder.

*A pleasant smile* will make your face look radiant. It's a form of beauty no man can resist and far outweighs the "perfect" mouth that does not smile. How

## Be A Woman!

many times have you seen a woman's beautiful smile
lift the spirits of those around her. A pleasant smile
is contagious. A smile does, of course, expose your
teeth. They should not be discolored and cavities
should be taken care of. (Irregular teeth can have a
special, even sexy, appeal.) Smoking is not only bad
for your health, but it also stains your teeth and
causes bad breath. The best, though not the only, way
to eliminate these problems is by not smoking—I don't.

*Good posture* makes a big difference in any type of
figure. Carry yourself as though you are the world's
most gorgeous woman . . . and to your husband you
are! A straight spine is better for your health, and it
also gives the body a better appearance. Standing tall
with shoulders back relieves pressures that cause
damage to the spine and internal organs. At the same
time, you create a stature that says "I believe in myself" and your appearance will be greatly improved.
Look as though you are proud of yourself—you
should be, because you are the queen of your castle
and the object of your husband's love.

*Your hair* should be kept simple. Men usually do
*not* care for anything extremely fancy. It should look
and feel like the "real thing." Many years of modeling
has shown me the value of healthy, shining hair.

Hair plays a big part in sexual attraction. There
have been cultures where the women traditionally
shaved their heads upon marriage so they would not
look so attractive to other men.

No matter what hair style you choose, the important factor to your husband is that you have clean,
good-smelling hair. Stiff hair from sprays, dullness
from lack of washing, and generally messy hair is a
turn-off to men. Another turn-off is wearing curlers
in public or in bed. Don't *ever* go out in public with
curlers. If you must use them when your man is

122

around, *be sure* to cover them beautifully with a well pressed, pretty scarf. Wash and set your hair while he is at work.

*Your eyes* are probably the most looked-at part of you. No matter what shape or size they are, they *can* be attractive. Mascara can enhance your eyes; it puts a twinkle in them and brightens and lifts your face. When using eye shadow, make sure you use soft pastel colors (I prefer off-white). Don't go by the make-up ads—they will sell you anything. If you have dark circles under your eyes at certain times of the month, use a cover-up or a very light shade of foundation on the dark part.

*Good skin* is important and an asset to anyone's beauty. I have seen models who seem to have fantastic skin as their *only* perfection. What a look of beauty it gives them. However, if you were not blessed with it, here are a few tips to create that illusion. If your skin is sallow, your husband will love the fresh glow a cream rouge will give, even if you don't wear another bit of make-up. The rouge should be applied as soon as you get up. It gives a soft and natural glow. Put a little on your lips, too. You will look fresh and alive when you send your husband off to work.

Dry skin needs a moisturizer applied each morning, no matter what else you do or don't do to your skin. Moisturizer helps seal in your own moisture while it protects the outer layer of skin from the sun, wind, dry air, and pollution. Your skin will stay younger-looking and softer many years longer. I know! I started using moisturizer night and day years ago, and my husband tells me today that my skin looks younger than my forty years. Your outer-skin layer changes every ninety days. So start now—it's never too late.

Washing oily skin with soap and water, as many cosmetologists once advised, can actually cause long-range problems. If you wash too often with hot soapy water, it dries the outer layers of skin and they will eventually begin to wrinkle. The best treatment for oily skin is to clean it with a nongreasy lotion especially made for oily skin. Or use *warm* water (not hot) and, with a soft cloth, rub *gently* over the oily areas. Apply witch hazel (or any astringent for oily skin) *only* over the oily areas. Then—very important —apply a light moisturizer for oily skin around your eyes, neck, and any area that is not oily.

Don't take normal skin for granted! Use a moisturizer and clean well at night.

Recommended for all skin types: drink six to eight glasses of water a day, and try to get seven to eight hours of sleep every night. Don't overexpose your skin to the sun. Clean skin well before going to bed and, of course, eat a balanced diet.

Whatever you do, don't let your husband be exposed to your beauty treatment! (I like Steve to think it's *natural* beauty.) If you need extra oil on your skin, give yourself a treatment while he is at work. If you only have nights to do it, keep your oil or cream under your pillow so you can apply it after the lights are off. It only take a second and you don't really need the light.

*Your hands* can be one of your beauty assets. Have you ever noticed Barbra Streisand's hands? They look so soft and she moves them so gracefully. Wearing gloves while washing dishes or scrubbing floors will protect your hands and prevent puckering and drying. But many women don't like to bother with them— too much trouble. If this is true in your case (mine, too), I'll give you a secret I've had for five years. Put A & D Ointment on the back of your hands whenever they feel dry. Then apply it all over your hands and elbows at night before retiring. The smallest amount goes a long way. If you can't get used to using such a rich oil, then at least use a rich hand lotion.

*Your nails* shouldn't be too long and they should be well kept. Most husbands don't talk to their wives about their nails but, judging from my research, they sure notice them. Keep them clean by using lemon juice underneath the nails. It helps to remove stains. Keeping a coat of polish on them can help prevent breakage. If your nails break easily, eat more protein and vitamins A, B, C, and D. Color polish is alluring to most men. But there are some men who don't like bright polish. Find out what your husband likes— he'll be happy to know you want to please him. If he says "whatever you like," then that's what he means. Don't pressure him—he has given you the choice.

*Your being overweight* might be pleasing to your husband, and if you are not unhappy with extra weight, then skip this subject. You only have to please your husband and yourself. For those of you who would like to lose weight, read on.

It is known that almost anyone who wants to lose weight can. There are very few people who cannot lose because of medical reasons. It's mostly psychological. In other words, *you* are in control. One of the homemaker's biggest problems is that she is home during the day (most of the time alone) and she often feels that cooking just for herself is not worth it. So she nibbles high-carbohydrate snacks all day instead of preparing an adequate lunch with proper nutrition.

First of all, you most certainly *are* worth it! And not only will you lose weight with a better diet, you will look better and feel better. Your husband will notice the total difference.

A few years ago, I took inventory of my diet and vitamin intake because I did not have the energy I wanted and needed. I have always prevented myself from overeating, but obviously I was not eating a proper diet. My inventory told me what to do. I cut way down on white sugar, used less salt, less bread, and ate more fresh vegetables and fruit. Then I added to my diet vitamins A, B, C, and E. Wheat germ, honey, and yogurt became part of my everyday diet. I kept carrot sticks, apples, and oranges in the refrigerator, ready for whenever I wanted to snack. Candy and most cookies were not on my shopping list. I did not cut down on butter, as the body needs butter (oil) for stronger, healthier hair and skin. Steve agreed to try my new diet as a lark, but was so pleased with the results that he decided not to go back to his old one. If you can convince your husband to try it for two weeks, he might see a change in his energy and general well-being. If he refuses, don't push it. Nothing is worth making his life unhappy.

If you have a lot of weight you would like to lose, check with your doctor first. Let him approve your approach. Then, once you get the go sign, do not allow *any excuse* to stand in your way. Become enthusiastic about your new venture—after all, you are about to become a new you. Ask your husband to join your new interest. He can be an added incentive and make your project more fun. Or you can approach your new venture as you would a secret surprise for your husband. Plan to become the weight you want to be for his birthday or a special occasion. Then work on it without mentioning it to him. What satisfaction you'll get when he starts noticing the new you!

If your husband wants to lose weight, be positive and support his attitude. If you keep cakes, candies, ice cream, white breads out of the kitchen, it will help him. Keep fresh fruit, carrots, celery, et cetera for him to snack on. Have dinner ready in the early evening, and you should both agree not to snack before going to bed. Eating then just gives all those calories a chance to turn into thick, fatty cells, instead of being used up for energy.

*Exercise* can be done in more ways than you might think. When I vacuum (not one of my favorite responsibilities), I think of the beauty it's giving to me. Did you know that vacuuming tightens the arm and stomach muscles? Knowing that is the only reason I don't hate vacuuming. If you have stairs in your home, using them will tighten your leg muscles. Bending up and down from the waist, which seems to be part of our everyday life, is excellent for the waistline. (But if you are bending down in public, remember to bend from the knees. It's more flattering.) I do as much walking as possible. I walk twenty blocks to a store and then back many times a week. You may not live that close to a store, but you can still make it a point to walk each day. Ask your husband to join you after dinner every night. Tell him your reason (more exercise) and suggest that it's good for him, too. Now, the trick is to walk with a long s-t-r-e-t-c-h-i-n-g stride, at a fast pace. Walking slow does not burn up calories, and a short stride does not stretch those muscles. If he walks with you, you have the added pleasure of those moments alone.

Gardening also has exercise advantages. Bending at the waist, sometimes at the knees, and digging in the earth are all very good for the body.

If you would like more exercise, take inventory of your husband's activities to see if you could join him for exercise and fun. Steve invited me to play golf with him before we were married. I was not too interested in golf, but I was interested in Steve. I took it up then and have been playing with him ever since. I'm not that good at it. When he wants a tough game or great competition, he plays against his male friends. But if he wants a game of fun, he invites me. And that's what we have—fun!

Maybe swimming, jogging, or playing tennis would interest you. Buy a badminton set and challenge the entire family to fun and exercise. Then, of course, there are the less fun ways to exercise. That is the rigid, well planned ten to twenty minutes of daily calisthenics. But if you can encourage your husband and children to join you, you can all have a lot of fun and laughs.

In *clothing* the first rule I follow is not to spend so much that I irritate Steve, because then he would begin to see the money spent instead of an attractive addition to my appearance. Overspending could become a burden to him and take away the element of a pleasant surprise.

Clothing does tell a lot about your personality. If buttons are missing or a seam is out, find time to repair it before wearing the garment. Clothes should always be pressed well to give a look of respect for yourself. Whether you wear blue jeans with a T shirt or an evening gown, they should be your type of clothing and not some fad that a designer has whipped up to sell to anyone with the money to spend. Your husband's opinion is more important than following the latest fad. Check with him—he's the one you are trying to please.

Keep your husband's wardrobe in good shape, too. Check for missing buttons and open seams. Keep checking to see if any of his clothing needs laundering or a visit to the cleaners. If he can't follow up on shining his own shoes, ask your children (if they are old enough) to do it. Your husband will appreciate it and your children will be learning respect and giving.

*Personality* should reflect the individual you. Proverbs tells us: "Her ways are ways of pleasantness, and all her paths are peace." And in Ecclesiasticus, we find: "The grace of a wife will charm her husband, her accomplishments will make him the stronger." Being attractive is only a part of your personality. Many of the most attractive people are not particularly good-looking; some even have physical defects. It is their personality that gives them their drawing power.

Your inner qualities are the keys to your personality: kindness, honesty, dependability, unselfishness, and sincerity all contribute to making you what you are. A woman with a quick temper or tactlessness displays an unattractive personality, and no matter what she looks like, people will find her unpleasant to be around!

It's worth every effort to make the most of the assets you have. The more you take care of yourself, the higher valuation your husband will have of you. You will *feel* more alive if you look more appealing, and your husband will love you more for taking the initiative to get more out of life.

# 7

# Self-expression

## Could Your Husband Be Bored with You?

When I was dating my future husband, I was never bored. Why? Because we did not have a *routine* together. In our early years of marriage, I was never bored either, because of the sheer novelty of new experiences. We shared a home; we made love any time we wished; I followed my husband's career with a hopeful eye. I have found that keeping the mind and body occupied has a great deal to do with keeping boredom out of our marriage.

But, as the newness wears off, where do you go? How can you prevent this terminal disease called *boredom*? When your home is "set" and your children need you less, and your husband's career is established in a predictable pattern—what then? You are now stripped of all your diversions. How many times can you redecorate the living room, even if he lets you?

You are now familiar to your husband and with him in every way. Nothing new any more! This certainly leads to boredom, not only for him, but for you, too.

Boredom is developed by boring people. If you are bored by someone, it's almost certain that you are boring him. The first thing to do about boredom is to

get out of your normal routine. You may be so involved with the pattern of home and children that you
may have forced some part of yourself underground.
Seek new interests and amusements and tell your
husband about them. Study your husband and note
what his interests are in *all* areas—sports, friends,
hobbies, sex, job—and carefully start catering to them.
He will begin to treat you as the most delightful person
he knows.

Remember always that *any* two people who live
together do get caught up in the routine of everyday
life. The excitement of your courtship and new relationship cannot last forever. But as long as you keep
yourself interested in something—almost anything
new—you will have this experience to share with your
husband so that he doesn't become bored with you.
It will keep his interest in you alive. But remember
also that your self-expression must *not* overtake your
responsibilities at home. Don't get so wound up that
you forget to keep things up on a daily basis.

I feel so strongly that "*de*boring" ourselves makes
for stronger and better marriages that I'd like to go
into the "how" of it a little more deeply.

## The Boredom Syndrome

Boredom is the most prevalent female affliction
today. With all the modern products on hand to save
her time, she is practically certain to fall prey to it.
Millions of women complain about boredom, but
many more millions do not complain about it—because they do not even know that that is what disturbs
them. So how can they expect their husbands to know
and understand them?

The consequences of boredom are more serious
than they appear at first glance. True, nobody ever

dies of it, but boredom is often the indirect cause of severe psychosomatic disturbances, some of which may surprise you—fatigue, simple aches and pains, and ulcers, which are often caused *not* by pressure but the lack of it. Bored people actually get sick just so they'll have something to do.

A bored woman is more apt to find solace in drinking; she can cause anxieties in her marriage; behind the wheel of a car, her mind often wanders. In fact, in extreme cases, she can become so depressed she develops suicidal thoughts.

Milder forms of boredom result in loss of interest and enthusiasm. It can also dull the intellect and cut down awareness.

One of the saddest things about it is that boredom breeds boredom: bored people usually make poor listeners and have little to say. This makes them rather uninteresting—and soon un-sought-after—companions. Bored people then shut themselves away, failing to meet the world halfway.

There is no reason why anyone—that's right, *anyone*—should be bored. Like smoking or drugs, boredom can become a habit, but only if you let it.

Remember: boredom is not an *external* problem. There is no such thing as living a "boring life." Boredom comes from *inside*. It is an excuse for not knowing what's going on in your mind. You don't have to become rich to shake off the boredom blues. You don't have to travel around the globe, entertain or be entertained by "beautiful people," or even become the life of the party. You *can* be *yourself!*

## How to Fight Boredom—Four Easy Lessons

Here's a profile of a woman who is *not* a bore:
1. *She is interested.* Not only in herself but the

whole world. Things. Issues. People. Her friends and —most important—her husband and children. Curiosity may kill cats but not people.

2. *She is involved.* Her interests go beyond watching TV soap operas every afternoon. Her church and her community need her and want her. She is *part* of what she is interested in.

3. *She is enthusiastic.* She has never lost the capacity to get excited. Did you ever watch interesting people respond to things? They can be like children. Good for them!

4. *She loves.* People. Projects. Her heart is as big as her mind. And she respects feelings, other people's and her own . . . . in short, *she cares.*

## You're Better Than You Think

Few people know the limits of their capabilities. The fact is we all have skills, strengths, special talents. Don't wait for others to bring the best out of you. It's up to *you* to discover your potentials and make use of them.

Your husband didn't marry a limp dishrag; he married a special woman—*YOU!*

## Stop the Boredom Habit

*Develop a New Interest.* There are many interesting things you can do to "debore" yourself. Things that are fun and interesting—chess, bird watching, bridge, church projects, walking, sightseeing, antiques, volunteer work, coin or stamp collecting, to name a few.

*Start a New Hobby.* If you can get your husband interested in your hobby, you'll have an opportunity to exchange ideas and thoughts. Or try a new sport.

Taking up a new sport will not only fight boredom, it will also help you stay in shape. Try one your husband is interested in, then you can have fun together. Don't take up skiing if he has a bad back or skating if he has weak ankles—the idea is to get closer to him.

Now don't say you have no area of expertise. Or that you could never be an expert on anything because you have never had the education, talent, or training. Nobody is born an expert; all it takes is getting interested in an issue or subject. Next, read all you can about it and ask people who are already experts on the subject to tell you what they know.

An expert is *anyone* who knows enough about a subject—no matter how small it is—to be a source of knowledgeable advice and help.

My sister Carmen is an expert on—would you believe it!—goats. She wanted fresh goat milk, so she bought a couple of goats, learned all she could about them, and began breeding them. Now she sells them, and people come to her for information on their care and on how to bred them. She also "invented" goat butter. It happens to be delicious. She sent the recipe for goat butter to a health magazine and had the satisfaction of seeing it published. She then began receiving letters from people who had tried it and wanted to thank her for sharing the recipe.

My father is an expert on the Bible and on good health. He combined the two and has written a book called *God's Food*.

It's exciting and interesting to know a lot about one subject. It can be about grasshoppers; it doesn't matter. I can think of several questions right now I'd like to ask an expert. How high can they jump? How old is an old grasshopper? How many babies do they have at one time, and how often do they give birth?

See—even a dumb grasshopper can use an expert to tell its history.

Maybe you already are an expert—on dogs, cats, birds, sewing, history, hair, flowers, fish, decorating, painting . . . Then you know all about the excitement that can come from just finding out about something— and sharing that excitement with your husband.

## Do the Unexpected

*Be a Miss Fix-it.* Who says women can't fix anything? If you can't complete it, ask your husband for help.

*Build Almost Anything.* Shelves, picture frames, lamps . . . Visit your nearest lumberyard for inspiration. Your husband will be proud of you—and you will save money, too.

*Be the First Interior Decorator on Your Block.* People will love you for it, especially your husband.

*Learn a Second Language.* Take your husband with you to the class. Then you have each other to practice with.

*Be a Volunteer.* There is a great need for women in volunteer organizations. As a matter of fact, some groups would fold if it weren't for the women who donate their time, energy, and intelligence to keeping them afloat. Furthermore, we all have an obligation to help others, and working at a hospital or for your church can give you enormous satisfaction.

*Improve Your Voice.* A woman should have a soft, feminine-sounding voice. Your voice should be as gentle as a caress when you speak. If it's not, try for improvement. Your husband will be grateful.

*Have a Garden or a Greenhouse.* Be Mother Nature. Your man will love the results. Put your own

fresh vegetables on the table or send him a plant from
your greenhouse for his office.

*Raise a Pet.* Anything that moves. Learn everything
you can about that pet. Children are very animal-
conscious, and raising a pet is a good way to teach
them a reverence for life.

*Take a Course in Make-up.* You're still a woman,
first and foremost. And one of your prime objects
should be to look good for your husband.

*Make Your Husband Love Your Cooking Even
More.* There are cooking schools aplenty. Varied
menus are a delight for the whole family.

*Design Your Own Clothes.* Or your children's.
Perhaps you already sew. Now start designing—you
*can* do it. The satisfaction will be tremendous, and
you can save your husband money, too. He'll be
impressed.

*Paint.* Not only walls and ceilings, but canvases.
There are no hard-and-fast rules to becoming an
artist. Had Grandma Moses ever been inside an art
school?

*Collect.* Anything at all. Bells, match covers,
menus, chess sets, buttons, old Valentine cards, bad
jokes, glass eggs, vases—even insults. Jot down everything you can learn about what you collect. Ask your
husband to get involved by keeping his eyes open for
additions to the collection.

*Join the Local YWCA.* Get in shape. They have
plenty to offer in physical fitness, sports, and education. And the Y is family oriented, so this can be a
togetherness activity.

*Learn to Play a Musical Instrument.* Not everybody
will be laughing when you sit down to the piano—
especially your husband. Perhaps you can learn together. Music is soothing, remember.

*Keep Up with the Latest Dance Steps.* It'll do

wonders for your ankles and figure, and add to your grace.

*Take a Course on the Bible.* Too many people forget that it's all been said before, and better. Reading Bible passages with your husband and children makes for a close-knit family.

*Rediscover the World Through Your Children's Eyes.* Museums, the zoo, the library—expose them to the world, and grow with them.

*Go on a Diet.* Tape a picture of yourself as a bride to the refrigerator door and vow to look once again like your husband's young love.

## Age Has Nothing to Do with Your Spirit

Unconsciously, many women put an age limit on certain abilities. Silly souls. Some girls are old ladies at twenty. Others retain their bounce at sixty, seventy, or more. Boredom is a state of mind, remember.

My grandmother is eighty-three years old and she has never allowed herself to be bored. I think the fact that she has always been involved and enthusiastic about life has kept her as agile as a young woman. My grandfather died many years ago; with no husband or children at home, she could have let herself go deep into boredom, but she didn't. Today, she drives her friends to the doctor, the market, or wherever they need to go. Most of them are younger than she. She goes to the beauty parlor one day and the next she's out planting her flower and vegetable gardens. Last year, she painted the outside of her daughter's nursery school. She also makes a lot of her own clothes and, of course, goes to church regularly. She gets up early in the morning and she's ready to go! At eighty-three she has no time to be bored. She has taught me a lifelong lesson: don't ever stop growing. Your mind is alive as long as you live.

## Be a Romantic

There is nothing wrong with having your head in the clouds—as long as your feet manage to reach the ground once in a while. Don't ever let anyone knock your dreams. Some of the best and most practical ideas started out just that way.

So let your imagination run loose. Dream of the painting you are going to paint, the pup you are going to raise, the quilt you are going to design. Then *do it!*

## I Can!

These are magic words. Powerful. Remember them. Scribble them on a piece of paper. Now frame your masterpiece and hang it up on the wall. Look at it every morning when you get up—a great way to start the day! There is nothing you cannot do once you set your mind to it. Human beings are marvelously adaptable, intelligent, persevering. And you're human, aren't you?

Repeat after me:

*I can learn*
*I can enjoy*
*I can create*
*I can love*
*I am never bored*
*The world is full of surprises*
*Something wonderful happens every day*
*I want to get the most out of my life—it's the only one I've got*

And you'll never have a dull moment. *Never*. And

your husband will always be wondering what exciting move you will undertake next. Your interests make him more interested in you. His love for you will stay alive because you will be more alive.

# 8

# I Vow as a Wife . . .

LIFE IS VERY short. Every morning God allows you to wake up you should vow to get the utmost out of that day. To enjoy the sunshine, the rain, a flower, your children, your husband, sex—*all* the things God gave to you.

VOW to make your husband happy; to be the perfect wife.

VOW to create a comfortable home filled with love and respect for your husband and your children.

VOW never to be confused about your place in God's scheme—your place as a woman.

VOW to treat your husband with dignity, to accord him the same courtesies you would a friend.

VOW to never complain, never nag, but always to discuss.

VOW to be flexible, to make your life accommodating to your husband.

VOW never to be so preoccupied with house and children that you never have a moment's thought for your husband.

VOW to keep yourself attractive to your husband.

VOW that your sexual relationship is not going to be dulled by habit and custom, that you are going to take the initiative to throw routine and familiarity out of your sex life forever.

VOW to have frank discussions every week with your husband—not only about what is most interesting and exciting in sex, but in *everything*.

VOW to be romantic *and* seductive.

VOW to make him feel important around the house by appealing to his masculinity.

VOW to worry about his health, but never to nag him about it.

VOW to keep his favorite food in the refrigerator, his newspaper beside the chair, and his personal belongings where he can find them.

VOW to send him flowers on his birthday or after a special night together, letting his office know he is loved at home—that he has a wife who cares. His self-esteem will go up even more.

VOW to bring him breakfast in bed once in a while.

VOW to be proud of who and what you are—a wife and a mother.

VOW to be a woman.

# Complete Woman Analysis Test

THIS TEST IS really designed to let you know what you can expect to learn from this book. Don't feel bad if you get a low score the first time you take this test. Take the test now—then take it again six weeks after you begin putting this book into practice. You will find that you will have increased your awareness of your relationship with your husband.

## Complete Woman Analysis Test

| Relating to Husband | Now | Six weeks from now |
|---|---|---|
| 1. Am I proud of my husband's masculinity? | | |
| 2. Do I know God's point of view about the male/female role? | | |
| 3. Am I constantly trying to change my husband's character? | | |
| 4. Do I let him know, in some way, every day that I love him? | | |
| 5. Do I think about and appreciate what it must be like to carry all the financial responsibility for a family for a lifetime? | | |
| 6. Do I harp on his idiosyncrasies? | | |

*Be A Woman!*

| | | Six weeks from now |
|---|---|---|
| **Relating to Husband** | Now | |

7. Do I let my children know by my own actions that their father is the head of the family and should be respected as such?

8. Do I tell my husband, by word and deed, that I like him the way he is?

9. Do I give him reassurance whenever he needs it—taking his side if possible?

10. Do I let my husband know that I need him in **every** way?

11. Do I let him know that I **need** him sexually?

12. Do I always support him in public?

13. Do I nag him?

14. Am I always trying to change him?

15. Do I encourage our children to help make him comfortable?

16. Am I always comparing him with other men?

17. Do I openly admire him?

18. Am I always polite to him?

19. Do I see him as my friend?

20. Do I tell him my positive feelings about him?

21. Do I know enough about his occupation to make him feel I really care about his career?

22. Do I talk about all my problems when he comes home?

# Complete Woman Analysis Test

| Relating to Husband | Now | Six weeks from now |
|---|---|---|
| 23. Do I invite his friends over as our guests? | | |
| 24. Do I keep up with his interests? | | |
| 25. Do I look for opportunities to help him out? | | |
| 26. Do I accept the fact that males and females think differently and should respect their separate God-given functions? | | |
| 27. Do I just **expect** my husband to support the family, without thanking him in some special way occasionally? | | |
| 28. Do I know what my husband likes most in the home? | | |
| 29. Do I ask my husband to sit down once a week with me so we can analyze how to improve our marriage? | | |

| Relating to Myself | | |
|---|---|---|
| 1. Do I read something new each week to be more interesting? | | |
| 2. Do I like and appreciate my female role? | | |
| 3. Am I too preoccupied with housework and not enough with my husband? | | |
| 4. Do I live each day as though it is my last? | | |
| 5. Do I consider my homemaking an occupation and know the value of it? | | |
| 6. Am I as organized as I can be? | | |

| | Now | Six weeks from now |
|---|---|---|
| **Relating to Myself** | | |

7. Do I keep a daily calendar to help me run a more organized house?

8. Do I set up impossible daily goals?

9. Do I know the value of a ten-minute nap each day?

10. Am I a procrastinator?

11. Do I know enough timesaving tips so I can be with my husband more?

12. Do I feel guilty **just** being a wife and a mother?

13. Do I know that being part of a man's life is being a more complete woman?

14. Do I know all the advantages of being born female?

| **Relating to Sex** |
|---|

1. Do I know why sex is good for me mentally and physically?

2. Do I know why God approves of sex?

3. Do I give the total responsibility of love-making to my husband?

4. Do I "give" my body, instead of always having to be "taken?"

5. Do I seduce my husband sometimes?

6. Do I know what turns my husband on?

7. Do I tell my husband when he pleases me?

| Relating to Sex | Now | Six weeks from now |
|---|---|---|
| 8. Do I know why I should never pretend an orgasm? | | |
| 9. Do I know where or when not to engage in sexual fantasies? | | |
| 10. Do I know the value of sexual communication? | | |
| 11. Do I know what the female sexual capacity is? | | |
| 12. Do I know all about the female orgasm? | | |
| 13. Should I be my husband's mistress? | | |
| 14. Do I know the value of sexual variety? | | |
| 15. Do I know what makes sex become boring? | | |
| 16. Do I know what to do to make the bedroom always look inviting? | | |
| 17. Do I know the value of varying lovemaking techniques? | | |
| 18. Am I willing to make love at unorthodox times? | | |
| 19. Do I know the aphrodisiacs of lovers? | | |
| 20. Do I think I'm frigid? | | |
| 21. Does my menstrual cycle or menopause have an effect on my sexual drives? | | |
| 22. Would I know how to handle my husband's impotence? | | |
| 23. Am I predictable or boring in bed? | | |
| 24. Do I read books and literature on sex? | | |

| Relating to the Total Relationship | Now | Six weeks from now |
|---|---|---|
| 1. Do I think of my husband as my friend as well as my provider and lover? | | |
| 2. Do I know the power of love? | | |
| 3. Do I know how to make his love last? | | |
| 4. Do I confuse emotional love, psychological love, spiritual love, and physical love? | | |
| 5. Do I value laughter? | | |
| 6. Do I know that tenderness, trust, and repect strengthen the relationship? | | |
| 7. Do I disregard my husband's privacy? | | |
| 8. Am I able to communicate with my husband? | | |
| 9. Do I know that too much complaining can undermine my marriage? | | |
| 10. Would a crisis strengthen my marriage? | | |
| 11. Do I know when and how I am unintentionally cruel to my husband? | | |